# NIETZSCHE: PHILOSOPHER AND POLITICIAN

ALFRED BAEUMLER

# Nietzsche

## PHILOSOPHER
## & POLITICIAN

ARKTOS
LONDON 2024

# ΛRKTOS

Arktos.com   fb.com/Arktos   arktosmedia   arktosjournal

**ISBN**
978-1-915755-85-8 (Paperback)
978-1-915755-86-5 (Hardback)
978-1-915755-87-2 (Ebook)

**Translation**
J. R. Sommer

**Editing**
Constantin von Hoffmeister

**Layout & Cover**
Tor Westman

# Contents

ৡ

# Translator's Introduction

ALFRED BAEUMLER'S introduction into English is long overdue. We might say this about any author whose works have somehow eluded translation, but in Baeumler's case it is especially true. Baeumler has been ignored — not because his work lacks merit — but because his side lost the battle in the great *spiritual* struggle that was World War II. Baeumler — along with Alfred Rosenberg, Richard Oehler, Ernst Bergmann, Carl Schmitt, and others — was a philosopher of the Third Reich; for this reason, the establishment — i.e., the bourgeois, "liberal-democratic" world-society established and perpetuated following the war — has chosen to ignore the thundering of Germanic history, no matter how significant. Victors write history, after all; and if the victors espouse liberalism, what do those they silence advocate?

Baeumler and his compatriots were conservatives — not in any modern sense, but in the *Nietzschean* sense: *We are Hyperboreans!* roars Nietzsche at the outset of *The Antichrist*. The Third Reich and its philosophers had a *spiritual, conservative*, and, yes, even *empirical* understanding of the world; this understanding was born in Nietzsche. Postwar interpreters have branded Nietzsche as a rebel championing the *progressive* individual, the "free spirit." As Baeumler shows, however, Nietzsche rebelled against the swelling, Enlightenment-spawned liberalistic wave because of its *destructive* drive — "progress," after all, means trampling that which precedes. Contrary to liberalism's crushing urge, the Third Reich was the logical conclusion of Nietzsche: preserve what deserves (empirical), center it on a myth (spiritual), ensure a better future based on principles of the past (conservative); the

Reich's very existence was the argument; the task of its philosophers was to articulate this.

Not wanting to grapple with the ramifications of a philosophy so injurious to the winning side, the postwar world recast Nietzsche as one of their own: *Nietzsche did not denounce the effects of the precious, cosmopolitan Enlightenment; his enemy was the anachronistic, nationalistic state* — so the modernists argue.

Nietzsche, after all, was too towering, too brilliant to be silenced, so just *reinterpret* what he said. Those following in his wake — the Germans who carried his torch, those contemporaneous with the Third Reich — *could* be silenced: they were *quacks*, they were *evil*; they were anything but reasoned voices, next in line from Nietzsche, describing the primeval, natural need for a people's self-assertion. *Ad hominem* attacks create nothing, however, and only demonstrate the true instincts of the victorious liberalists.

The same modernists reinterpreting Nietzsche like to emphasize Baeumler's critics — Heidegger being principal among them. After all, if Heidegger considered Baeumler "an upside-down Ludwig Klages" with an absence of "actual philosophizing," then why pay attention at all to what Baeumler thought?[1] Herein lies the problem: Heidegger's disagreement with Baeumler was one of execution, not substance. What Heidegger loathed in Baeumler was only what he loathed in everyone who wasn't Heidegger: the inability to separate the institution from the spirit. For Heidegger, one of the most profound acts is for a healthy man to contemplatively visit a cemetery; his standards were quite lofty, if not visionary, and anything short of a spiritual revolution shorn of all mundane trappings — e.g., *institutions* — was failure. Baeumler — as chair of philosophy and political pedagogy at Berlin's Friedrich-Wilhelms-Universität, and tasked with institutionalizing a frenetic revolution — had no chance at earning Heidegger's sympathy, despite the two philosophers' substantive ideological overlap. In fact,

---

1   *Ponderings II–VI* (Indiana University, 2016), "Ponderings and Imitations III" (Fall 1932), §207, translated by Richard Rojcewicz.

Heidegger believed Baeumler to be quite capable and "clever." But this hardly matters to modernist reinterpreters; Heidegger, with his staggering brilliance, is useful to them when he slights their foe. Beyond this, he must be ignored. But what is it the reinterpreters ignore? *Substantive overlap*: Heidegger: "*Globalism*: the last step of the machinational essence of the power to annihilate what is indestructible on the path of devastation. The 'modern' human being is on the verge of making himself a slave to the devastation."[2] *Enslavement* to a lie — this is the great fear of the philosopher of *Dasein*; Baeumler, like Nietzsche, shared this concern: "Those who have money participate in rule, those who do not belong to the millions of slaves of the plutocratic system.... Modern democracy is in every way a system of absolute duplicity — it is *compulsion* with a veneer of 'freedom'" (p. 165). But Heidegger had more to say that resonated with his fellow German philosophers:

> The question of the role of world-Judaism is not a racial question, but a metaphysical one, a question that concerns the kind of human existence which in an utterly unrestrained way can undertake as a world-historical 'task' the uprooting of all beings from being....[3]

Ernst Jünger, one of the few thinkers Heidegger seems to have openly respected, likewise faces reinterpretation: his *On the Marble Cliffs* (1939) is incessantly presented as *the* critique of the Third Reich. Never mind his voluminous interwar writing praising the advent of, as Baeumler put it, a "new order" (see Appendix):

> A real revolution has not happened yet, but its marching step can already be heard! This is not a reaction, but an authentic revolution with all its telltale signs and slogans, its idea is the *völkisch*, sharpened to an unprecedented edge, its banner — the swastika, its political expression — the concentration

---

2    *Ponderings XII–XV* (Indiana University, 2016), "Ponderings XV," 206.

3    *Ponderings XII–XV* (Indiana University, 2016), "Ponderings XV," 191.

of *will*, a dictatorship! It will replace word with *deed*, ink with *blood*, empty phrases with *sacrifices*, the pen with the *sword*.[4]

What is at stake in the modern world, despite the protestations and obfuscations of the reinterpreters and ignorers, is — *being, spirit.* The point of such obfuscation is to distract: *don't look at the existential problem confronting you, look at the petty squabbles amongst kinsmen instead, look at what* we *want you to see* — so say the liberalists and globalists. Baeumler, Nietzsche, Heidegger, Jünger — each in his own way held fast to the truth of a metaphysically (and thus physically) damning present and future. Fight for your future now, or serve as your own finale.

Baeumler's apparent censoring represents not just a revision of German history, but of European history in general; however, his blatant omission from history does a disservice to Germanic (i.e., *European*) people everywhere: one of their voices has been silenced for an agenda that seeks their eradication. But this is also an affront to *thinking* people everywhere. As Carl Schmitt rightly observed: liberalism feigns tolerance until actual decisions must be made; then, the sovereign inherent in any governing system steps to the fore. No ideology — not even a liberalistic one in all its avarice, perhaps even *especially* not a liberalistic one — can tolerate dissent: "*gold's imperialism does not tolerate any other point of view*" (p. 171). "Under the guise of humanitarian phrases hides the most *unrestrained veneration of violence* world history has ever seen" (p. 164): The modern Western world order reveals its inner sovereign through *ad hominem* attacks, ostracization, censorship, sanctioning, *silencing*. This, however, as Schmitt also noted, represents the deceptive tendency tacit in "tolerant" systems. This dishonesty is *unnatural*; and such *unnaturalness* is

---

4    Jünger, "Revolution and the Idea," *Völkischer Beobachter* (September 1923). For recent treatment of Jünger's thought in light of the Hitlerian era, see Martin Friedrich's *Hitlerism* (Clemens & Blair, 2023).

the target of all illiberalists. This is why Baeumler's work is relevant today.

Once and for all, Baeumler makes plain the spiritual-revolutionary pulse threading Nietzsche's philosophy, and Nietzsche spoke for all European — i.e., *Germanic* — peoples.

Alfred Baeumler was a German and, as such, was more of an authority on Nietzsche — his kinsman — than any of the sanctioned interpreters before or after the war. Excepting Heidegger's exegesis, the West has enjoyed a dearth of *German* interpretations of the great German, Nietzsche. Karl Jaspers, for example, had no interest in seeing Nietzsche for what he was (his Germany was hostile to his anti-Germanic ideology, just as he was hostile to it); Nietzsche, for him, was ultimately something of a schizophrenic; thus, he sought to subvert any meaningful interpretation of the philosopher of the *will to power*, considering him merely an unsystematic, albeit incisive polemicist. Karl Löwith, a student of Heidegger and brilliant scholar in his own right, was *not* German, despite his birthplace. And while Löwith presents the best non-Germanic interpretation of Nietzsche, it falls short of demonstrating the connections Nietzsche so plainly made. Thomas Mann, a spiritually and morally bankrupt deviant, could claim German blood, but nothing else; Mann embodied liberalism's *will-to-Nihilism* to his very core and was thus fundamentally at odds with Nietzsche's *Weltanschauung*. Walter Kaufmann, liberal academia's standard bearer for Nietzsche scholarship, was Jewish, not Germanic; his scholarship is rife with unscrupulous bias; Kaufmann's goal was to appropriate Nietzsche from the Germans and turn him into a cosmopolitan "free spirit," a task at which he was undoubtedly successful; taking Kaufmann's interpretations as authoritative, however, is like presuming a scholar from the Congo is the appropriate authority on the Talmud; some Talmudists might object to this. Baeumler, on the other hand, sees in Nietzsche what Nietzsche saw in himself and in the world around him: Nature always has the final say.

Central to Baeumler's interpretation is Nietzsche's *illiberalism*. Nature, of course, is always illiberal: it rewards the strong and crushes the weak. Man has *subverted* Nature with his liberalism, which is the spiritual successor of Christianity, and is thus living counter to natural law; hence we hear Nietzsche lambast the notion that evolution leads to *improvement* — the notion is naught but progressive, liberalistic fantasy: "The species do not grow in perfection: the weak prevail over the strong again and again, for they are the great majority..." (*Twilight of the Idols*). The "weak majority" has done nothing to deserve the power liberal-democratic societies (ostensibly) give it. And even if the "weak majority" is merely a manipulated tool of the governing "progressive" elite, this only highlights another of Nietzsche's critiques of liberalism: it is *dishonest*.

Under the banner abstractions of *equality, justice, liberty, tolerance*, etc., the governing elite galvanize the unwitting masses into a progressive frenzy — willing even to tear down their own approved history — for the sake of keeping "the people" marching ever "forward." What this translates to in practical terms, however, is a *progressively* indoctrinated citizenry alienated from its roots and thus conditioned for perpetual state-subsidization — so long as it conforms with state mandates. An indoctrinated, subsidized citizenry is docile, content; it is a "tolerant" society that stands for nothing except the protection if its own *selfish* interests within the idoctrinating system; it will not threaten the governing elite's power. This, of course, is precisely the kind of state Nietzsche so fervently railed against: it is not the state *qua* state, but the liberal (Christian) state that softens and, ultimately, kills a people. "*The idea of tolerance is the contradiction of justice*: it abolishes the contradiction, it confuses the order of things, because it names the struggle as something that is to be condemned" (p. 44). Baeumler saw this plainly in Nietzsche, where so many of his contemporaries and successors did not — their exegeses "conformed with state requirements." The liberal interpretation of Nietzsche demands an atomized world of "free spirits" — each, in turn, demanding their own "unique," customized experience. This aligns with the overarching liberal strategy of creating a society of de-*communitized* consumers, all forever groveling over and voting for the approved progressive agenda, and all easily governed in the name of their banner abstractions — Nietzsche would call this *enslavement*. The subtitle of Nietzsche's *Human, All-Too-Human* was *A Book for Free Spirits*: "The word 'free spirit' in this book must not be understood as anything other than a *spirit* that has become *free*, that has once more *taken possession of itself*."[5] Nietzsche cared not a whit for the "mob" of supposed "free spirits" — he believed in destroying systems that have only ever enslaved and alienated peoples from their roots. Freedom for Nietzsche, as Baeumler argues, is *knowing thyself* as part of a *healthy whole* ("I purged myself of everything that was foreign to my nature"). Baeumler's exegesis comes from another time, another world, a more Germanic world, the world from which Nietzsche himself spoke.

*Struggle* was the only reality for Nietzsche. His entire being was set on reorienting the Germanic people back toward their pagan, pre-Christian roots, and one of the principal steps to achieving this was a general acceptance of heroism, honor, bravery, and war. As with Heraclitus, war, for Nietzsche, was the father of all things. Thus, to reject war is to reject its progeny — for good and ill. The liberal state's (un)natural conclusion is a conformist, atomized consumer society wholly averse to war (for, ostensibly, war disrupts the economy and is "morally" abhorrent; in reality, however, wars are often pursued in liberal-democratic states for elitist profiteering). Here, the terrible consequences of war are eliminated — yet so are the great, uplifting consequences: fidelity, community, heroism, honor. From these worthy consequences, greatness flows, genius is born. For Nietzsche, struggle is the means to greatness, culture, and power. Baeumler, more than any philosopher since translated into English, understood Nietzsche's aim: "Nietzsche [developed] ... *the first philosophical system to overcome the*

---

5   *Ecce Homo*, "Human, All-Too-Human."

*mechanistic worldview that has prevailed since the Enlightenment*" (p. 21). Nietzsche teaches us: "Men are *not* equal: thus speaks justice." Baeumler shrewdly adds: "Inequality and struggle are the prerequisites for justice…. Justice can only exist where forces are measured against each other in *freedom*. Under an absolute authority, in an order of things that a divine Lord knows, in the realm of the *Pax Romana*, there is no longer any justice, because there is no longer any struggle" (p. 41). A world without struggle leads to "a fictitious harmony, … a world without forces and opposites" (p. 45); from here, chaos ensues. This fictitious harmony has *tolerance* at its base, but tolerance rejects both justice and even humanity — because it rejects the conditions Nature imposes. The liberal *Weltanschauung* is inhuman not only because it will lead to societal collapse, but also because it will only generate nihilistic alienation along the way: in short, it dehumanizes.

The founding father of this liberalism that is "Germany's doom" (p. "In summary: Nietzsche fights against the "Reich" — not because it is German, but because it is German and Christian. With its Christianity, Germany, for whom Nietzsche would like to provide spiritual guidance in Europe through his philosophy, is committed to those tendencies that are driving towards decline. In vain has he shown how corrosive Christianity is in its modern, dissolved form in all areas of life and spirit. He pointed out the disastrous consequences of the concepts of equality and justice — but the German spirit, which just now had the will to rule over Europe, the power to lead Europe, "under the pompous pretext of establishing a Reich, justified its transition to mediation, to democracy and 'modern ideas'…" "Decadence reaches so deeply into the value-instincts of our politicians, our political parties: they instinctively prefer what dissolves, what accelerates the end." The German Reich is but one of the "half measures" of modern democracy. In order for there to be institutions, there must be a kind of will, instinct, imperative, "anti-liberal to the point of malice" — but instead of the "will to tradition, to authority, to responsibility for centuries, to the solidarity of gender roles forwards and backwards in infinitum" the new Germany has the will to doom: it is liberal." on page 119) is Bismarck. Baeumler recognized both that Bismarck hadn't the spirit of the Germanic people as his core interest, and that Nietzsche's frequent rebukes of the state stemmed exclusively from his detestation of the Bismarckian "Reich": this "Reich" was no community of Germanic people — it was a liberal construct meant to pad lifestyles. Bismarck's state "is just a breeding ground for herd animals" (p. 59). Amidst this headlong rush to ruin, Germany's chancellor fails see the importance of the world-historical moment: instead of leading Germany to assume its role as the spiritual-political leader of Europe, Bismarck simply satiated the progressive profit-lust of the moment; the "Reich" was handed over to "democracy and 'modern ideas'" (p. 118). Thus the way is paved for Nietzsche's "future European": "the most intelligent slave-animal, very hardworking, very modest, excessively curious, pampered, and weak-willed, with cosmopolitan passions..." (p. 127). Nietzsche's goal, then, Baeumler soundly contends, is "to prevent the worse from reigning because the better stand aside out of disgust" (p. 129). Nietzsche sounds the alarm for those who listen with "good ears."

Yet, Baeumler goes on to argue, Nietzsche is not against the state *per se*. Instead, Nietzsche's "disgust was aimed at the Roman-Christian form of decay of the state" concomitant with liberal-democratic governance (p. 131). If established from a spiritual-conservative foundation — with meritocratic, Napoleonic sensibilities — a state is necessary: "The state as an *heroic* phenomenon, as a system of rule, as a source of all great things, as a means and expression of the struggle for the highest power, which is *never* merely physical or economic — *that is a Germanic conception of the state.... The state exists where there is greatness, where a bold leader commands valiant men and pursues far-reaching goals*" (p. 132). Be heroic, conserve and be loyal to what warrants conservation and loyalty, and, above all, recognize enslavement in "progressive" veneer as pernicious. Throwing in your lot with the liberal state is the gateway to international socialism — known today as *globalism* — and to the slave-society *par excellence.*

Few have recognized Nietzsche's true meaning as Baeumler has. I hope that in a more just — i.e., *freer* — future, Alfred Baeumler will be seen as the masterful interpreter of the great German he was. Maybe in this *freer* future the real Nietzsche — "the Siegfried-attack on the urbanity of the West" (p. 132) — will be revealed.

჻

Two additional treatises appearing here for the first time in English are Baeumler's "Nietzsche and National Socialism" (1934) and "World Democracy and National Socialism" (1943). These provide essential context for Baeumler's thoughts on all three topics, which he believed to be inextricably intertwined. The former further marks Nietzsche as a prophet of National Socialism; prophecy can only be understood in retrospect, and Nietzsche augured what the Great War generation experienced first-hand. The latter essay is an important discussion on the relationship between *absolute peace* and *absolute power*. If peace is sought, power is necessary; this, of course, can only lead to "inhuman" conditions. More than mere indictment of the Versailles Treaty, it builds upon a Nietzschean framework of *power* to critique the Western idea of *peace*, examines what the contradiction inherent in this idea means for the future, and proposes a "more human" alternative to democracy's absolutism when the contradiction is removed.

J. R. Sommer

2024

# Translator's Note

GIVEN THE VARYING TRANSLATIONS of Nietzsche's work, for simplicity's sake, I have indicated individual passages or aphorisms in his writings with the "§" marker. Additionally, I have identified my footnotes with "[trans.]" — all other notes belong to Baeumler.

For transparency on certain nebulously translatable words, I have added the German term in brackets. I translated such terms according to context.

Finally, I take full responsibility for all translation shortfalls, should any be identified. And I hope Baeumler's work will continue to generate able, reverent treatment.

# Author's Foreword

IN THIS WRITING, Nietzsche is treated as a *European* thinker and placed alongside Descartes, Leibniz, and Kant. He himself had not really read Descartes, Leibniz, or Kant; he only understood the systems of these thinkers in their connection with the Christian tradition and thus opposed them. What matters is not the accuracy and wealth of his historical *knowledge*, but the extent and meaning of his historical *existence*, which deals with those systems.

You will not find the vivid language in my portrayal that one is used to from others. However, we are not dealing here with the poet and writer, but with Nietzsche the philosopher and politician. Anyone who projects the writer's variegated statements onto a single level and then tries to unite them, in turn, within a single level of interpretation can only arrive at a unified picture by making Nietzsche inconsistent. The real unity of this well-hidden man and his work is revealed only to those who know the foreground and background, polemics and philosophy. I believe my interpretation clarifies a few main concepts and thereby says something remarkable about the last of the great European thinkers.

The two aspects, *philosophy* and *politics*, do not indicate arbitrary veins through Nietzsche's work, but are necessary starting points for a methodical interpretation of the overall appearance. In discussing Nietzsche as *philosopher*, I limit myself essentially to epistemology and metaphysics; I am not concerned with comprehensiveness, but merely with clarifying Nietzsche's unity of thought. Application to individual areas of the human-historical world — such as the conduct of life and education, art, psychology, philosophy of history — would be a task in itself.

I tried to uncover the floorplan of a buried temple and stacked some column drums on top of each other. I hope that others will undertake reconstruction of the complete building.

Dresden,
Alfred Baeumler
January 1931

# Author's Introduction

Up to now, Nietzsche has always been understood — and misunderstood — from the basis of Christianity. He was accepted as the perfecter of Eckhart's or Luther's work; he was understood as a prophet, a believer, or at least someone who struggled to believe. Even his atheism and his hostility to Christianity were only seen from this point of view: he was just an apostate, and the more violently he declared himself against everything Christian, the more his inward confession of faith was believed to be belying his certainty. The religious interpreted his life as the passion of the wicked and his suffering as the result of unbelief. The secular, on the other hand, found this suffering inspiring, the outbursts of solitude intoxicating.

We cannot go into the misunderstandings to which Nietzsche's life's work is exposed. Part of the reason for the improbable scope of these misunderstandings lies in the nature of the work itself. Nietzsche's published writings do indeed show very different faces, and, while it is not impossible to see the unity of his life's work from them, if one adds the unpublished writings, the unity of Nietzsche's production quickly becomes clear. One sees a writer who blazes his trail with the greatest certainty from the beginning — albeit without knowing it himself. At first it may seem as if he was enthusiastic about art, science, Greeks, and saints, always extreme, always faithless, just as fervid in exhilaration as in condemnation. As if the man, who exemplified loyalty to a great task like no other, had played the flippant role of a lyrical-ecstatic Judas! How does it look in reality? During the period of his most exuberant hopes for Wagner and the coming German culture, the young

Nietzsche wrote the harshest psychological truths about Richard Wagner with his incisive pen — a few years later, during the period of his psychological and skeptical aphoristic books that were so cold and dismissive, he does not give up his highest hope. Nothing is one-dimensional with him; he is never a mere brooder, an aesthetic experiencer. A hidden will directs his steps. Every single work he publishes pursues an exacting intent: with each tome the author wants to meet and convince certain people, to produce a specific effect. Therefore, each of the works has a different tone, sound, and style. Every book is an artistically stylized action; it turns against someone, against something, and can only be properly understood from this point of view. So one cannot simply infer Nietzsche's "views" from these works. Just as the intention demands, the author shifts between light and shadow: he praises where, in truth, he knows he is superior — yes, he even praises the enemy; he stings and mocks those with whom he agrees. But this never happens arbitrarily: everything is determined by the *one task*. What he actually wants, he always only gives a hint. What he gives immediately is always foreground; he is a master of the foreground. He can be so because he is unshakably certain of his background. Nietzsche writes, as it were, pseudonymously: Schopenhauer, Wagner, Dionysus, the "free spirit," Zarathustra — these are all fine masks.

Nietzsche knows how to make effective use of momentary moods and ideas, impressions and experiences. But what is central is always the hidden pathos of his being. There is something uncanny about the art with which he knows how to hide, with which he creates foregrounds around himself. Sometimes he is afraid of "this whole uncanny, hidden life" that he leads.

Many bright colors and lights play on such a work; this is due to the sensitivity of its author — but at the same time it is a product of art and will. The colors are chosen and applied with wisdom; a unity of essence, a unity of will is hidden behind it. If one does not see Nietzsche's *essential task*, his vision dissolves into lyrical fragments and aphorisms. But to whom this matter has come to light (and this is where the difficulty lies), the Nietzsche phenomenon is clear. Nietzsche and his cause are one; unity, not multiplicity, is the character of his life.

Europe has been under pressure for centuries, as if it has been looking in vain for something since the end of the Middle Ages: a form of life, a lost unity and security of existence. This Europe is called *Christian*; but everything else is possible: Greek and Roman, Indian and Chinese, philosophical and aesthetic, scientific and technical, war-like and mercantile. In fact, it does not itself know what it actually is, and therefore anxiously and restlessly searches for forms and concepts in all times and cultures. The people of this Europe live in a thousand uncertainties and contradictions. Everyone tries to come to terms with himself in his own way: one kneels before the sacraments, as did the people of the Middle Ages, the other tries to refresh his Protestantism with modern ideas, others throw themselves wholly into the arts or scientific asceticism. Political and social "problems" arise — no one overlooks them, yet no one can make sense of them.

A man separates himself from the sunlit crowd, which, working, babbling, and enjoying themselves, stands out against the dark wall of clouds of an uncertain future. Only one sentence comes from the lips of this man with the prescient eye: "God is dead." He does not say: *there is no God*. He says: *God is dead*. He says: *God is no longer believed*. Modern man is a chaotic mess; he no longer has a unified soul — if he believed in God, this chaos would not exist. But chaos is there — so God is dead. Nobody pays attention to the speaker; his closest friends think he is a fool. "The greatest events are hardest for people to feel: for example, the fact that the Christian God is dead, that in our experiences there is no more heavenly goodness or education, that there is no longer divine justice, no more immanent morality at all. It will take a few centuries for Europeans to feel this terrible reality: and then for a while it will seem as if all the stress is gone." That is Nietzsche's experience: things have lost their focus. This is Nietzsche's horror: nobody notices it, nobody sees the terribly vast emptiness. The old values have been given an additive that makes them worthless — but that scarcely bothers the citizens. You only find that values themselves have become "problematic." Everything turns into a problem; God himself becomes an idea, sometimes even a problematic idea. The less one believes, the more one speaks of God. A silver-tongued religion or even rambling religiosity has taken the place of silent belief in God. Then someone appears who is too proud to turn unbelief into a "religious problem." He has the courage to look into nothingness, he has the strength to ask: *What now?* What inexpressible folly to speak of a "prophet" in view of this unique situation — as if there could be a prophet without a God whom he proclaimed. It is true that Nietzsche was sometimes tempted to become a martyr, a sacrifice to God. He invented Dionysus: *Dionysus versus the crucified*.[1] But he also found the role of *prophet* to be ridiculous and must therefore be separated from the feeble myth-makers.

If one wants to historicize Nietzsche's appearance, one must simply say that *it means the end of the Middle Ages*. The Middle Ages only came to an end with Nietzsche, and the fact that this has not yet become known is the basis of all the misunderstandings that Nietzsche's appearance still meets. The outcome of the actual Middle Ages, viewed in depth, is followed by only two events: Reformation and Counter-Reformation. What follows from these two movements and what apparently heralds a "new era," Enlightenment and Romanticism, merely repeats these two movements: the Enlightenment is daughter of the Reformation (with a prevalence of congratulatory gushing), and Romanticism means a resurgence of the Counter-Reformation. (That is, *Romanticism* as a spiritual-political movement in Europe, which had and still has the restoration of the Christian state as its goal.) Do not object to German Classicism [*Klassik*][2]: this Classicism is only a moment between the Enlightenment and Romanticism — a

---

1    This is the last line of *Ecce Homo*. [translator]

2    The *Sturm und Drang* movement lasted from circa 1760s-1780s. Weimar Classicism lasted roughly from 1772–1805. Hamann, Goethe, Herder, and Schiller were prominent figures of this period. [trans.]

subjective event, not a spiritual-political one; an event of form, not an event in the reality of things, therefore also without consequences and without transformative power. The German bourgeoisie, which took this event as real and historical, does not collapse today by chance... Nietzsche means the end of the Middle Ages: he is neither enlightener nor Romantic. He stands beyond the two camps and is therefore understood by the epigones of neither. The supporters of Romanticism, the defenders of the Christian-Germanic state, perceive him as an apostate and rebel — at best as a tragic revolutionary; those in the Enlightenment camp claim him as a standard-bearer of progress and as a European stylist — a free spirit. But if something can be proven with either interpretation of his work, it is that both are wrong: he is neither a random denier of God and a revolutionary — his awareness of the historical moment is too sharp for that, his realistic prudence too great — nor is he an enlightener in any form; he is not a moralist, humanitarian or pacifist. He throws himself violently against both aesthetic and political Romanticism. In democracy, however, he saw his real opponent — because here, under the cover of scientific and political slogans, he recognized the *more modern and therefore more dangerous form of Christianity.*

As far as the Christian culture of the West reaches, so does the official validity of the concepts of love, compassion, and tolerance derived from it. The meaning of the Enlightenment is based on the fact that through it the concept of *caritas*[3] was transferred into the secular. Nietzsche fought hardest throughout his life against Rousseau, against the century of the Enlightenment with its intellectual and moral optimism, with its sentimental belief in the harmony of reason, virtue and luck, and its tendentious philosophy of tolerance. So goes the sketch of *The Will to Power* — we good Europeans are waging a war against the 18th century.[4] This war against the 18th century is only

---

3    That is, *Christian love of humankind; charity.* [trans.]

4    *The Will to Power*, §117.

the negative side of the philosophy of *The Will to Power*. Up to now, this destruction has been viewed too myopically — Nietzsche's fighting position has been seen in isolation, without reference to the vast background of metaphysics. Even *Thus Spoke Zarathustra* should only be seen as a preparation for his main metaphysical work! This major work presents the world in precise visions before us. *The Will to Power* is a real philosophical system, a strict connection of thoughts — but the "rigor" is not to be sought in the logical interlinking of the parts, but in the inner coherence and consistency of the whole. Nietzsche thought intuitively — each of his ideas is an intuition; each of his concepts comes from the heart; each of his thoughts is a spark from the same glowing center. Nietzsche's work was a gathering of such sparks. When he returned from his lonely walks, or on the way, he wrote down his intuitions with a swift pen. The rest was just editing. Nietzsche was not familiar with problems that one locked up in cages and fed every day in order to observe them. If you want to judge his work, then you have to take on the logical task of putting it together, for which he had no time. The decisive factor for the assessment cannot be formal perfection, but only the inner context of the concepts. The pre-Socratics also left no elaborate systems. What is decisive, however, is that the context of the terms is present and can be brought to a logical clarity at any time.

This philosophy is unknown, even its name is unknown. It was obvious to Nietzsche to speak of a "Dionysian" philosophy. But his main philosophical work and his teaching are more correctly named after a Greek philosopher who really lived than after a god invented by a philosopher in need: not *Dionysian*, but *Heraclitic* — this is what we call the image of the world Nietzsche saw. It is a world that never rests, *becoming* is everything; but *becoming* means *fighting and conquering*. "War is the father of all things," spoke Heraclitus of Ephesus; he was the thinker whom Nietzsche felt from the beginning to be a spiritual forebear, and whom he has most venerated at all times of his life. To see the world and people in a Heraclitic way means for him to see them as they are: unexhausted and inexhaustible, creating and giving birth from the depths of the unknown; giving birth to shapes that arise from the cauldron of existence according to a law of eternal justice, fight one another, emerge victorious or perish. If one wants a formula for this worldview, it should be called *heroic realism*.

# I. The Philosopher

## 1. Realism

Once you said God when you looked upon distant seas; but now I taught you to say *Übermensch*.

God is a conjecture; but I do not wish your conjecturing to reach beyond your creative will.

Could you create a God? — Then, be silent about all gods! But you could well create the *Übermenschen*.

— "On the Happy Isles"

NIETZSCHE IS the first great philosopher of realism. Think not of any conceptual realism, nor even an empiricism or sensualism of any kind — how far is Feuerbach[1] behind Nietzsche! — rather, it is an original realism, a realism that begins a new phase in European philosophy. This realism comes from Nietzsche's ultimate depths — where the concept of the *Übermensch* rests. Because the *Übermensch* is a realistic conception, he makes sense of the earth. "The *Übermensch* is the meaning of the earth." From "unearthly hopes"[2]—this notion should return to areas of life and creating. "The heart of the earth is

---

1   Ludwig Feuerbach (d. 1872) was a German philosopher most associated with his stance that God is a subjective projection.

2   This and the preceding quote come from *Thus Spoke Zarathustra*, "Zarathustra's Prologue," which will hereafter be annotated as *Zarathustra*. [trans.]

of gold."[3] The term *Übermensch* is a formula for the attitude of heroic this-worldliness [*Diesseitigkeit*], an attitude that is not yet characterized when it says, "Love this life with all its suffering." *The heart of the earth is of gold*: This is the great faith of existence that expresses belief in the world, which is always only a reflection of a belief of the individual and his historical mission.

The this-worldliness of Nietzsche's philosophy must be seen as one with its heroic aim. This is Nietzsche's *Germanism*, which in his case is not only expressed in the political sphere: this philosophy is heroic and worldly [*diesseitig*] at the same time. Nietzsche is not a free-spirited atheist: he knows the "god-building instinct," though he admits this instinct sometimes comes to life in him "at the wrong time."[4] He denies this instinct. There is something in him that forbids him to speak of God today. *God*: today that means the degradation of man, the indebtedness of his will, the abolition of all virtues. That is why Zarathustra must be godless: *because the earth must be regained.* "There are a thousand paths that have never been walked, a thousand vigors and hidden islands of life. Man and his origins [*Menschen-Erde*] are still inexhaustible and undiscovered. — Watch and listen, you lonely ones! From future winds come furtive flappings; and good news flows to fine ears. — All gods are dead: now we want the *Übermensch* to live."[5]

Zarathustra sets out to fight for the earth; his undertaking is heroic, his soul is heroic. "What qualities must one have in order to do without God — what qualities for the 'religion of the cross'? Courage, sternness of the head, pride, independence and hardness, determination — no brooding." In the age of science it is man's honor not to believe in God; conscience and honesty demand it of him. European morality itself, which grew out of the belief in God, turned against this belief at its height.

3    *Zarathustra*, "On Great Events."

4    *The Will to Power*, §1038.

5    *Zarathustra*, "The Bestowing Virtue."

Nietzsche's realism is a consequence of truthfulness and courage. On its flag it is written: *Error is cowardice.*[6]

Nietzsche finds his philosophy as a hero, as a lonely fighter fated to a lost position. Perhaps there was only one of his contemporaries who felt similarly — it was no coincidence that the philosopher of new realism grappled with this thinker as he did with hardly any other. In the notes that Nietzsche's friend, the church historian Franz Overbeck, made and in which he tried to demonstrate the incompatibility of Christianity with modern scientific culture, there is also a section on Bismarck's religion. We read: "As a rule, Bismarck proudly kept silent about his religion with the self-loyalty that is characteristic of great people — most expressively in his 'thoughts and memories.'" Overbeck finds a hint of this hidden religiosity in the letter Bismarck wrote to his wife when he entered the diplomatic service (1851): "I am God's soldier. Wherever he sends me, I have to go, and I believe that he sends me and will use my life as needed." Here, Overbeck adds, we can look into the roots of his religiosity — "his religion sat in the soil of his self-esteem..."[7] The self-esteem of heroic natures is one with fate. Nietzsche's *Ecce Homo* arose from the same sense of self and self-confidence.

"A humanitarian God cannot be *shown* from the world we know: you can be forced and driven to this conclusion today. But what conclusion do you draw from this? 'He cannot be proven to us': the skepticism of knowledge. You all *fear* the conclusion: 'the world reveals to us a completely different God, one who is not humanitarian' — and, in short, you bond to your God and invent a world for Him that *is alien to us.*"[8]

It is the pathos of realization that drives Nietzsche to proclaim the "death of God." The world in which we live and the Christian God are in contradiction to one another — so the world and knowledge must

---

6   *The Will to Power*, §1041.

7   Franz Overbeck, "Christianity and Culture."

8   *The Will to Power*, §1036.

give in, concludes modern man. So the idea of God has to yield — concludes Nietzsche. He wants to free the world from the curse befalling it. This curse has been reduced to a formula by the philosophers: our world is one of delusion and deception; behind it lies the world of things in themselves, the true world. The former is a world of the senses, of appearance and becoming; the latter, a world of reason, truth and being. To expose the "true world" as a fiction — that is Nietzsche's concern as a philosophical thinker.

## 2. Being and Becoming

The task is to restore the real world, a *restitutio in integrum* [total reinstatement] in every sense. Nietzsche fights against *Eleatism*,[9] whose greatest propagator was Plato. "Christianity is Platonism for the people," says the preface to *Beyond Good and Evil*. Plato is separated from the older Hellenes by the lack of the idea of *becoming*. You see everything being rigid: They believe they are doing a thing an honor if they "dehistoricize it," if they consider it *sub specie aeterni*,[10] in short when they *mummify* it. This is their "Egypticism." Plato has strayed from the basic Greek instincts; he is under *oriental* influences: he turned the philosopher into a "conceptual idolater," i.e., a variety of the priest. The senses, "which are otherwise so immoral," deceive us about the real world: hence the philosophers put a world of ideas in their place.[11]

"I take aside, with great reverence, the name of Heraclitus. If the other philosopher people rejected the testimony of the senses because they showed multiplicity and change, they rejected their

---

9    That is, *Eleaticism*. Parmenides founded the Eleatic school, which favored reason over sense experience in pursuit of truth. Zeno of Elea, part of the school, famously revealed paradox in the everyday. [trans.]

10   That is, *under the form of eternity*, or, more clearly, *from the perspective of eternity*. [trans.]

11   Nietzsche, *Twilight of the Idols*.

testimony because they showed things as if they had duration and unity." Heraclitus also did the senses injustice: the senses do not lie at all. *We* first put the lie into it, e.g., the lie of unity, of *thing-ness*, of substance, of duration. It is with precisely the "reason" of which we are so proud that we falsify the testimony of the senses. The senses show us the *becoming*, the passing away, the change — but that is the reality. So do not lie. "But Heraclitus is eternally proved right that being is an empty fiction. The 'apparent world' is the only one: the 'true world' is only a lie …"[12]

Nietzsche takes the side of "error" in favoring the *senses* and *becoming* against the truth of *reason* and *being*. It did infinite harm to his great conception that he could not get rid of this opposition in the presentation of his basic idea — because this led to his always speaking of "error" where he meant the truth. This fact is to blame that one could see in him a skeptic, a relativist, a philosopher of the "as if." Anyone who wants to understand his philosophy must know how to abstract from his polemics some of the main concepts. When Nietzsche takes the side of error, he means the "error," i.e., what the idealistic philosophers *declare to be error*. But that is precisely the truth! Through our senses we have access to the world itself. Our body recognizes things as they are in itself because *it* is a thing in itself.

In innumerable passages of his works Nietzsche pointed out the anti-Christian, anti-Platonic, and anti-idealistic character of his teaching. All of our philosophy, he says, has *theologian* blood in it. The instinct and arrogance of theologians are at work wherever one claims the right to "consider reality and look alien." The idealist, just like the priest, has all the great concepts in hand and now plays them against the senses and knowledge.[13] Christianity is a form of mortal hostility towards the realist.[14] Idealism is the heir of Christianity: the

---

12 Nietzsche, *Beyond Good and Evil*.

13 *The Antichrist*, §8.

14 *The Antichrist*, §27, §30, §47.

idealist escapes from reality.[15] It is morality derived from Christianity, the "Circle of Philosophers," which leads thinkers astray. It has always been important for them to save the freedom of will, to see people as *responsible.* An "instinct to punish — and to judge" lurks behind this wish — the psychology of free will is an invention of the priests. It is based on a wrong interpretation of what goes on in us when we "want" something. We believe that we are the cause — we mean "to catch the causality in the act." For the perpetrator, however, we consider our consciousness, the "spirit," our I, the "subject." Such an assertion would of course presuppose that our will, our consciousness, is able to move something. But this is a mistake! The will moves nothing, it only accompanies processes; but it can also be absent.[16] If this is not recognized, then all processes are understood as an act (of man or of God), everything that happens becomes an act, i.e., it becomes the consequence of a will and thus loses its innocence. In the place of the real flow of events, we now believe we are seeing "things" — which are only structures of our consciousness that shifts its own identity *into* the flow of events, creating "things" that do not even exist. The resting, "being" thing is a fiction, a fiction of consciousness. There are no identical things, everything is in flux. Self-identical consciousness creates these things in its own image. It is we who have created the thing, i.e., the same thing, the subject and the predicate, the doing and the object, the substance and the form. "The world *seems* logical to us because we have first *made* it logical."[17]

This is essentially Kant's teaching: understanding dictates the laws of Nature. But with one crucial difference: Kant believed the flow of events was disorderly, senseless and worthless, that the categories of the mind first shape the sensory material captured in space and time and thereby create meaning and order. Nietzsche, on the other hand,

---

15  *Ecce Homo,* "Why I Am A Fate."

16  Nietzsche, *Twilight of the Idols.*

17  *The Will to Power,* §521.

seeks the categorizing [*Logisierung*][18] we undertake with the world as a necessity imposed with our existence, as a kind of poetry to show our imagination. The logical processing of reality is only a condition for us to live in this world, to be able to find our way in it. Admittedly, Kant is not far from this opinion either: in the *Critique of Judgment* he repeatedly emphasizes that it is only "our" (human) understanding with which the criticism is focused. But the opposite lies in the fact that Kant seeks all knowledge on the path *away from* the senses, while for Nietzsche the senses, the living body, *are* the real instruments of knowledge. Therefore he can recognize the categorizing [*Logisierung*] of the world as our achievement, but he has to evaluate this achievement differently than Kant. Consciousness presents us, says Nietzsche, a "world of identical cases" — but precisely with this it removes us from reality. By thinking we do not *fix* the "true" world as a connection of concepts, types, forms, purposes, laws, but we merely *make up* a world in which our existence is made possible. "We are creating a world that is predictable, simplified, understandable, etc. for us." Forms, types, laws, ideas, purposes — these are fictions; we have to be careful not to accuse them of a "false reality" — because then we imagine that the event "obeys" these forms, laws and ideas, while it is autonomous [*selbstherrlich*] and innocent! We carry an artificial division into what is happening, a division between what is doing and what is being done — but no factual situation corresponds to this separation of the *what* and *after-what* [*wonach*]. It was invented so that we can see something permanent in what occurs, because the form, the law, is something permanent and therefore more valuable. But the form is just invented by us — life flows ceaselessly among all forms, and no matter how often "the same form is reached," that does not mean it is the same form — rather, something new always appears.[19]

---

18   Or "making logical," a *logicizing*. [trans.]

19   *The Will to Power*, §521.

It is important to hold onto this aspect: there is nothing remaining in the real world to which we can cling, the stream of events rushes unstoppably through us and past us. This world is a world of passing away; it takes strength to endure it. The image of an "existing" world filled with standing forms arises from a decrease in this strength. Whoever resolutely asserts himself in this great growth and decay by organizing the world around him can withstand the gaze into the *becoming*. Whoever lacks this power adds a meaning into becoming that exists in itself—because then he does not need to create it. The Heraclitic world is thus the *contradiction* of a strong will: "He who is unable to put his will into things, the man without will or power, at least puts a meaning into it, i.e., he believes there is already a will in it. — It is a measure of *willpower* — how far one can dispense with the meaning in things, how far one can endure living in a meaningless world: *because one organizes a small part of it oneself*."[20]

From this summit we take a look at the last peaks of Nietzsche's thought-landscape [*Gedankenlandschaft*]. As a student of Heraclitus, he destroyed the world of *beings*. He has proven that it means a decrease in power when one puts a will, a purpose into the event, when one accepts a God who *gives* the event a meaning: but in doing so he has turned all values around, he has affirmed and deified *becoming*, the "apparent world" approved as the only one. Now what is the truth, the will to truth? Truth cannot be an awareness of something that is fixed and determined in itself, something that we only have to take in and grasp. Truth only exists for us insofar as *we* fix something, create boundaries, define something in the *eternally flowing*. "The will to truth is to *establish*, to *make permanent*, to *remove false character*, to *reinterpret into being*. 'Truth' is therefore not something to be discovered — but something to be *created* and that gives the name for a process, or, better yet, for a will to overcome, which in itself has no purpose: to put truth into it, as a *processus in infinitum* [infinite

---

20   *The Will to Power*, §585.

process], an active determination, — not an awareness of something that is fixed and determined in itself. It is a word for the 'will to power.' Life is based on the presupposition of a belief in the permanent and regularly recurring; the more powerful the life, the broader the world of knowledge and being must be."[21]

## 3. Consciousness and Life

What do we imagine follows from an "active determination," an "overwhelming" and "creating"? This question is at the center of Nietzsche's epistemology. Consciousness does not determine and create, it is the living body [*Leib*] that does this. The living body is of an older nobility than consciousness, even with regard to recognizing. All errors of previous epistemology are based on the fact that cognitive function has been ascribed to consciousness, while it really belongs to the living body. Man *feels* as a unit before he becomes aware of a unity. If I have something of a unity in me, says Nietzsche, it is certainly not in the conscious self and *feeling, willing, thinking*, but somewhere else: it is in the preserving, appropriating, eliminating, and supervising cleverness of my entire organism, *of which my conscious self is just a tool*. The I-feeling must not be confused with the "organic sense of unity." The order we bring about through our concepts must not be confused with the much older order that arises through the activity of the ensouled body. "We were creators long before we created concepts." The concept is subsequent to the form, the picture precedes abstraction. "Man is a creature that creates forms and rhythms; he does nothing better, and it seems nothing pleases him more than inventing forms." Our perception is an original appropriation; the essential occurrence in it is an *action*, even an *imposing of forms*. We are *active* down to the bottom of our perception, "only the superficial speak of 'impressions.'" Man recognizes rejecting, choosing, shaping. "There is something active in the fact that we accept a stimulus at all and that we accept it as such

---

21  *The Will to Power*, §552.

a stimulus. It is part of this activity not only to set forms, but also to assess the created structure in terms of incorporation or rejection. This is how our world — our entire world — comes into being." And to this world that belongs *to us alone and which we have first created* corresponds no *thing-in-itself*, but only our reality. Knowledge is an expression of the basic organic function of the assimilation drive. The essence of abstraction does not consist in omitting, but rather in underlining, emphasizing and reinforcing.

Nietzsche does not deny the activity of consciousness. He also describes it in such a way that the difference between this activity and the basic cognitive function becomes clear. The logic, he says, is linked to the condition: "Assuming there are identical cases." But Nietzsche does not draw the conclusion from this that there is *another* kind of active determination, overpowering and creating forms, than the organic-sensual one; he can rather be moved to this assertion: reality is "falsified" by this assumption. This "forgery" could also mean creating sensory images! The word has no sense because there is no such thing as a "true" world. Here Nietzsche is seduced by the desire to completely suppress the consciousness that other philosophers have so massively overestimated. He would have to recognize two kinds of abstraction, two kinds of unity, two different functions of knowing. But he probably touches on the insight that thinking is an analysis as opposed to "creating," but he does not explore it. Instead, he tends to think of the "small reason," that is, what we usually call *intellect* or *reason*, as arising from the "great reason" of the *living body*. The unity of consciousness would therefore only be a derivative of the organic feeling of unity. I attribute this error, among other things, to the tremendous impression that Darwin made on Nietzsche. This error is the source of his biologism, i.e., his tendency to trace everything, including consciousness, back to life processes. However, consciousness is not to be understood as a function of life; it is of a different nature from life; only if it is opposed to the flow of events can there be any knowledge at all. Nietzsche touched on this idea too, but he did not develop it.

For him, everything depends on using the living body and its meaning also for the recognition of its rights. Anyone who has to some extent considered the complexity of the living body—how many systems work there at the same time, how much is done for and against each other, how intricate are its internal processes, etc. — will judge that all consciousness, in comparison, is something poor and narrow: that no spirit is even remotely sufficient for what the spirit would be able to achieve here …" So, he concludes, we have to reverse the hierarchy: everything conscious is only of secondary importance, the spiritual is only a "sign language of the body."

The world of the spirit would therefore be a symbolic representation of the world of the living body. In addition, Nietzsche has another view, according to which the spirit is to be seen as a means and tool in the service of the higher life, the exaltation of life.[22] Two thoughts are opposed here: the spiritual as a symbol and the spirit as an instrument of the living body. Only in the second view appears what Nietzsche really cares about: the degradation of the conscious mind in favor of the unconscious activity of the living body. This tendency culminates in the finding that all conscious doing is more *imperfect* than the unconscious. "All perfect action is unconscious and no longer wanted; consciousness expresses an imperfect and often pathological personal condition…"[23]

This epistemology is characterized by the turn against consciousness. The meaning of consciousness has been overlooked by some philosophers; with Nietzsche there is no *over-seeing*, but a turn *against* consciousness. He allows another unit to take the place of the unit of consciousness and actually implements this basic idea. Behind the turn is his whole worldview, his world-transfiguration. This realistic doctrine of knowledge is directed against the "priestly and metaphysical

---

22   *The Will to Power*, §664.

23   *The Will to Power*, §289.

*hereticizations"* of the senses,[24] which replaces the Kantian "unity of apperception" with the whole human body. This living body is more than a work of art, it is an *artist*, a unit that creates forms and rhythms. Nietzsche develops the entire theory of knowledge from a transcendental aesthetic of the living body — transcendental logic takes a back seat. But one does not believe that this is why this epistemology can be dismissed as an aestheticism! What connects the cognitive creation of the body with art are the senses and shape. It does not follow from this that cognition is "only" an artistic process (even if Nietzsche's disregard of logic could lead to such a conclusion), but it follows that in the construction of the living body, in the activity of the artist and in the activity of cognition, the same organizing force expresses itself. Nietzsche expresses his sympathy for the artists loud and clear, but only because they are more right than the idealistic philosophers. "In the main, I agree with the artists more than all the philosophers up to now: … they did not lose the great trail on which life goes, they loved the things 'of this world' — they loved their senses."

In terms of the history of philosophy, Nietzsche's turn against consciousness is the most emphatic attack on Cartesianism in modern philosophy. (In this respect, too, Nietzsche again takes up Ludwig Feuerbach's struggle.) Descartes is the progenitor of idealistic philosophy, and the following sentence has been in force ever since: the idea we have of our soul is more certain and clearer than that which we have of our body.[25] Kant does not maintain this distinction, but he goes even further in the direction he has taken when he equates the external, physical appearances with the internal psychic ones, insofar as both are only phenomena and say nothing about the nature of things in themselves.[26] The distance that Descartes placed between soul and body [*Körper*] is placed by Kant between soul and body on the

---

24   *The Will to Power*, §820.

25   *Principles of Philosophy*, I, 8.

26   *Critique of Pure Reason*, 2nd edition, §68f.

one hand, and things-in-themselves on the other. Without knowing it, Nietzsche follows Kant's criticism when he puts the inner and outer world on the same level and emphasizes the phenomenality of the inner world.[27] Only the word "phenomenality" no longer has any meaning for him, because he is an idealist. Basically he just wants to say: the inner world has priority over the outer world, there is no distance from things-in-themselves, because there is no longer an ego that separated us from the living body and from the world. Where there is an ego, there is also a "body" as something alien to the ego. It is not by chance, however, that Nietzsche does not speak of the body [Körper], but of the living body [Leib].[28] The body [Körper] is the de-soulled living body [Leib], which is opposed to the abstract unity of consciousness; the unity of the living body, on the other hand, is the *will to power*. Only since Descartes founded the philosophy of consciousness has there been a "body" for philosophers. Nietzsche abolishes the philosophy of consciousness and restores the doctrine of the unity of the living body, which is fundamentally Greek. "Essential: start from the living body and use it as a guide. It is the much richer phenomenon and allows for clearer observation. Belief in the living body is better established than belief in the spirit."[29]

Nietzsche's epistemology is the most important achievement of anti-Cartesianism in modern philosophy. Anti-Cartesian trains of thought have often been heard before him; basically all empiricists are enemies of Cartesianism. However, Nietzsche is no ordinary empiricist. His realism is not based on the assertion that all of our knowledge begins with experience, but on the demonstration that the living body is a

---

27  *The Will to Power*, §477.

28  From Thomas Ots, *Embodiment and Experience: The Existential Ground of Culture and Self* (Cambridge University, 1994), 116: "German language knows of two different terms to refer to the body: *Körper* and *Leib*. *Körper* ... refers to the structural aspects of the body.... In contrast, the term *Leib* refers to the living body, to my body with feelings, sensations, perceptions, and emotions." [trans.]

29  *The Will to Power*, §532.

unit superior to consciousness. The empiricist is refuted by Cartesian philosophy before he begins. Nietzsche, on the other hand, gained a foothold at a point Cartesian philosophy did not reach. Of course, he has not always escaped the danger that threatens all anti-Cartesianism. When the "soul" is released from its connection with "God," when consciousness no longer takes the dominant position that the idealist gives it, then man falls back into the cosmos. The task would be to define it as a cosmic being, without allowing it to vanish into space, to see it in the context of Nature, without drawing false conclusions from the idea of its "smallness" in comparison with the size of the world outside of it. Quantity is not decisive. For the idealistic philosopher, the predominant position of man within the physical world is secured from the outset by qualitative, different, incorporeal consciousness. But as soon as the point of view of consciousness is given up, the question arises as to what still distinguishes man from other beings. He, who was just the "lord of creation," is now being swallowed up by the *Abyss of Things*, by the cycle of becoming and passing away.

Nietzsche realized this consequence of anti-Cartesianism very early on. The *Nachlaß*[30] fragment entitled "On Truth and Lies in the Extra-Moral Sense"[31] begins with the characteristic words: "In some remote corner of the universe, shimmering in countless solar systems, there was once a star on which clever animals invented knowledge. It was the most haughty and mendacious minute of 'world history': but only a minute." All the conclusions that result from the relativization of man to a cosmic being are drawn here with merciless consistency. Since the intellect is seen only as a "means" for the preservation of the individual, the drive to truth appears to be a riddle. The riddle is solved by Nietzsche's definition: to be "true" means to lie in a mutually beneficial style. Truth is defined as a "sum of human relations." It

---

30  The unpublished collection of writings discovered after Nietzsche's demise. The principal work in this collection was posthumously published as *The Will to Power*. [trans.]

31  1873.

is disputed that the conception of the world that man has, compared with that of the bird or the insect, should somehow be called "more correct," since there is no basis for this. We produce the ideas of space and time with the same necessity with which the spider spins; we do not know any other world than ours. Equalizing man's worldview with that of any animal seems to be the necessary consequence of every anti-Cartesianism. Nietzsche never fully refuted this consequence. Here is the expressive aphorism in which the sigh sounds: "Our uniqueness in the world! Oh, it is a very improbable thing!" — and in which the drop of life in the world is called meaningless for the entire character of the vast ocean of growth and decay. Yes, here you can even find the phrase about the "living rash" of our planet. "Perhaps the ant in the forest imagines just as much that it is the goal and intention of the forest's existence as we do when we almost involuntarily link the end of the earth to the demise of mankind in our imagination."

The relativism that speaks from these statements is of course not based on a failure of Nietzsche's intellect, but is more deeply founded. We are dealing here with the cardinal problem of philosophy, with the question of man: how is this question answered by a thinker who keeps his eyes on eternal growth and decay? You see, the followers of Cartesianism will shout, man and truth are perishing, Nietzsche's philosophy refutes itself! Such a conclusion would be premature. Let us not forget that Nietzsche's epistemology is only fragmentary. If we want to pass judgment, we have to interpret the fragments: such a test shows that a relativistic conclusion by no means has to be drawn from Nietzsche's starting points. His main thoughts can be accepted without the human being vanishing in space and the concept of truth losing its meaning. From a legacy that dates back to *The Joyful Wisdom* era and which is offered with the keyword "main thought!", it emerges that Nietzsche rose to a height of objectivistic thinking in some moments in which all relativistic impulses died out. In the first part of the mentioned note, the thought is repeated that there is no individual *truth*, only individual *errors*; yes, the *individual himself* is called an error. Then Nietzsche continues: "But I make a distinction: the imagined individuals and the true 'life systems,' each of which is one of us; — one throws both into one, while 'the individual' is only a sum of conscious feelings and errors, a belief, a piece of the true life system or many pieces thought together and wired together, a 'unity,' which does not stand up. We are buds on a tree — what do we know of what can become of us in the tree's interest! But we have a consciousness as if we wanted and should be everything, a fantasy of 'I' and everything 'not-I.' Stop feeling like such a fantastic ego! Gradually learn to throw off the supposed individual! … Beyond 'me' and 'you'! Feel cosmic!"

From this opposition of the "imagined individuals" and the "true life systems" follows a different conception of the human being than the relativistic one that always has the individual in mind. This is also indicated by the closing words "feel cosmic." "Wonderful discovery: not everything is unpredictable, indeterminate! There are laws that remain true beyond the extent of the individual!" The return of all human doing and driving, all action and invention to life processes does not have to be a destructive conception — it depends on what one understands by "life." Regarded as a cosmic fact, life would resist any relativization. If, of course, it is only understood as an empirical fact, as the biologist does, then Nietzsche's philosophy must appear as a single, immense biologism. Such an interpretation becomes completely unlikely, however, if one considers the meaning of the term "life" in the rest of Nietzsche's work. As can be seen from countless passages; "life" for Nietzsche does not mean something empirical-physiological, but something altogether *metaphysical*, even "Dionysian," i.e., a *divine phenomenon*.

## 4. Perspectivism

If there is a thinker besides Heraclitus who comes close to Nietzsche's philosophy, it is Leibniz. The system of the *will to power* is built on a monadological basic view: the world consists of a sum of units of power, from the conflict of which an equilibrium is established every moment. Each unit of power conceives the world according to its own measure — thus, there is no binding "truth" for everyone. In place of a static truth for all, there is a general dynamism and *perspectivism*. The truth dissolves into an unmistakable multitude of perspectives from individual power-centers. Even the Leibnizian definition of the monad as a *miroir vivant* [living mirror] is once used by Nietzsche (unbeknownst to him): "We are living mirror images." In the *Nachlaß* there is a description of Leibniz in which he appears almost as Nietzsche's double: he is called *dangerous*, a real German who needs foregrounds and foreground philosophies, daring and mysterious.

Leibniz created the system of pre-established harmony: each monad is a substance in itself and yet at the same time included from the beginning in the universal system of the highest wisdom and goodness. It is a wholly active power – but there is never a fight between these individual powers, because the substances do not touch: they are in a preceding harmony with one another.

Conversely, with Nietzsche *struggle is the only reality*; balance, harmony — these are the problem. Its system is monadological, but not harmonious. It means the tremendous attempt to understand everything that happens, all movement, everything becoming as "a determination of degree and power relationships, as a struggle."[32] In this respect, Nietzsche's teaching stands opposite Leibniz's as the last great attempt to justify the Christian God philosophically at the other end of the spectrum.

We have to distinguish between two types of relativism. Biological relativism speaks of the "environment" of a particular living being or a species of living being; it relativizes the individual and his world with regard to the existing greater world. This relativism can be found in Nietzsche, but it is negated by a deeper and more fundamental relativism, according to which the whole world is naught but a set of actions.

---

32  *The Will to Power*, §552.

The organic being is no longer helpless and small in the face of the immense, soulless universe, but its life represents a special case of what is going on in the world in general. This opens up the possibility that organic life is accorded a peculiar dignity: it is conceivable that in the organism the general essence of the world is most perfectly represented. Conclusions concerning the problem of knowledge can also be drawn from this. Nietzsche did not draw these conclusions, however; his epistemology is a torso.

Since we only know the world from our individual point of view, we fall into error after error if we consider our perspectives to be "true," i.e., generally *binding*. "Our world" is nothing but appearance, it is something that is brought about by the *creative* in us. Everything living has such a creative center, and everything that is in its "outer world" represents only the sum of its valuations. But these valuations are in some way related to its conditions of existence; they are "physiological demands for the maintenance of a certain kind of life."

Every single being is surrounded by an "apparent world" that is created by its valuations. The philosopher still recognizes this world as real, i.e., as belonging to total reality. The distinction between a "real" and an "apparent" world consequently loses its meaning for him.[33] Individual existences with their perspectives form "the world."

"Each center of force has its perspective for the rest of the world, that is, its very specific valuation, its type of action, its type of resistance.

---

33   It has been established that Nietzsche took the terms *real* and *apparent world*, *perspectivism* and *semiotic knowledge* from the book by the philosopher Gustav Teichmüller, which bears the title *The Real and Apparent Worlds*. However, this does not suggest that Nietzsche is dependent on Teichmüller in a substantive way. The book mentioned appeared in 1882. Already in his "On Truth and Lies in the Extra-Moral Sense" (1873) a relativism is sketched containing a germ of Nietzsche's later perspectivism. No doubt Nietzsche owes Teichmüller's book an acknowledgment, though substantively, he comes to opposite results. His reference to Teichmüller's formulations will not surprise anyone who knows Nietzsche's methodology: he always trains his sights on someone; he is always in a fight.

The 'apparent world' is thus reduced to a specific type of action on the world, starting from a center. Now there is no other kind of action: and the 'world' is just a word for the overall play of these actions. Reality consists exactly in this particular action and reaction of each individual against the whole… There is no longer a shadow of law left to talk about appearances here…"[34]

The *being* is that which acts on us, that which proves itself through its work. "It exists" means: I feel as if I exist in it.

For Nietzsche, "appearance" is only a word for the reality related to a subject, i.e., for the "real and only reality of things." The word *appearance* means nothing more than the inaccessibility of this reality for logical procedures and distinctions. The appearance is only appearance in relation to the "logical truth," which is only possible in an imaginary world.

For Nietzsche, the concept of appearance is therefore a consequence of his realism. "I do not set 'appearance' in opposition to reality, but, conversely, take appearance as reality which opposes the transformation into an imaginative 'truth world.' A certain name for this reality would be 'the will to power,' so designated from within and not from its incomprehensible fluid, protean nature." The *will to power* creates the world anew in every moment, interprets it anew every moment. It appears most powerful in organic beings: "The essence of organic beings is a new interpretation of the event: the inner multiplicity of perspective, which is itself an event."

"The interpretative character of everything that happens. There is no event in itself. What happens is a group of appearances, selected and summarized by an interpreting being."

The reality that concerns us, then, is the result of interpretation. Finally, the Kantian critique of knowledge comes to the same conclusion. With Kant, however, it is *reason* that interprets, with Nietzsche it is the *living force*. That does not mean a difference in degree, but a

---

34  *The Will to Power*, §567.

difference in essence. Because reason is only one, and this one reason corresponds to the one world of science. Nietzsche, on the other hand, tries to understand the real world, and he finds that there is no world without specific forces, each of which has its own specific way of reacting: a world without action and reaction would just be another word for *nothing*.[35]

But how is knowledge still possible in such a world? Doesn't everything here dissolve into actions of specific — i.e., unrecognizable — forces? Every being is absolutely active, every being interprets on its own and is therefore blind to the others: in this way do we not fall into the abyss of agnosticism, which is the necessary result of animal limitation?

We are faced with the core question of the philosophy of the *will to power*. The fragmentary nature of the work becomes particularly painful at this point. At least one of Nietzsche's answers can be reconstructed with the help of the rest of the *Nachlaß*. One must never forget that even in the apparently obscure field of epistemological criticism, Nietzsche always has an opponent in mind. If this opponent is logical idealism and optimism, then Nietzsche must be the conduit of relativism. This relativism does not arise from a desperation at the possibility of knowing, but is an honest reaction to the falsities of the philosophy of consciousness.

The philosophy of consciousness has logicized[36] [*logisiert*] the world; it has placed a network of concepts over reality and thereby hidden it from our view. In place of eternal becoming, it has put a fictional, rigid being. In the logically made-up world there are only relationships in themselves, relationships of dependency, which are formulated in the so-called "Laws of Nature." When two phenomena invariably follow one another, we assume a causal relationship between them, and unnoticed, this relationship, this "law," takes the place of the reality of

---

35   *The Will to Power*, §567.

36   That is, "made logical," or *categorized*. [trans.]

these two phenomena and their sequence. We substitute a ratio for reality and now believe that we will see the "same phenomenon" the next time on the basis of this formula. But with this we have deprived the real event of its uniqueness and unrepeatability, we have interpreted it from the outside, not from the inside. We call an "external" behavior a mechanical one: what is only regulated "mechanically" is only regulated externally. The whole mechanistically interpreted world presents itself to us as "externally regulated." Nietzsche, the philosopher of the *will to power*, who sees the world from within, must become an opponent of the mechanistic explanation of the world. Indeed, this is where the tremendous importance of his system lies: *it is the first philosophical system to overcome the mechanistic worldview that has prevailed since the Enlightenment.*

All movements, all appearances, all laws, it says in *The Will to Power*, are symptoms of an internal process.[37] The "law," which describes a regular occurrence, says nothing about the reality of the whole phenomenon: it only raises the question of *where it comes from* that something is repeated; it is a presumption to which the formula "a complex of now unknown forces and force-releasing" corresponds.[38] To assume that forces here obey a "law" would mean to deprive the event of its innocence, because the term *law* has a "moral connotation." It is something completely different from obeying: "the unalterable sequence of certain phenomena does not prove a 'law,' but a power relationship between two or more forces."[39] "The degree of resistance and the degree of superiority – that is what happens in everything… There is no law: every power draws its final consequence at every moment. The fact that there is no other way is precisely what makes predictability possible."[40]

---

37  *The Will to Power*, §619.

38  *The Will to Power*, §629.

39  *The Will to Power*, §631.

40  *The Will to Power*, §634.

Nietzsche does not deny the possibility of a certain pre-calculation of an event; he only denies the existence of "laws." Because with the term *law* one thinks of a lawgiver who demands obedience and of one who obeys out of respect for the law, as it were. A rigid, constant world also corresponds to the law: nothing new is possible under the law. The real course of events brings something new at every moment: "In no moment is oxygen exactly the same as in the previous one, but something new: even if this novelty is too fine for all measurements…" There are neither fixed forms nor fixed qualities: "The tree is something new in every moment: the form is asserted by us because we cannot perceive the finest, absolute movement: we put a mathematical average line into the absolute movement…" In the place of the law there is not lawlessness, but the "average line"; in the place of the "truth" comes "probability." "There are no more 'things in themselves' than there can be 'absolute knowledge.' Instead of basic truths, I put basic probabilities — provisionally accepted guidelines, according to which one lives. These guidelines are not arbitrary, but according to an habitual average. *Getting used to it* is the result of a selection made by my various desires, all of which wanted to feel good and endure." According to the above-mentioned aphorism of *The Will to Power*, we are allowed to expand this thought beyond the scope of the organic being: there are indeed no basic truths for the entire event, but basic probabilities, i.e., the event does not obey any "law," but, since every power draws "its consequence" at every moment, certain uniform outcomes arise again and again. We just must not assume that the same thing "happens" a second and a third time: *the outcome is always new.*

Life, the *will to power*, takes a new turn every moment. Individual events do not close together like links in a chain, but follow one another freely like throws in a game of dice. When Nietzsche lets probability take the place of truth, he does not put an indefinite chaos in the place of order, but replaces a wrong concept of order with a more correct one. His philosophy rejects the concept of an exact predictability of events; it claims that our knowledge of Nature is only a prediction of probable outcomes. In place of an allegedly causally determined world is set a world of events that follow one another, independently of one another, purely "randomly," just like the aforementioned dice throws. We know this randomness also has its order: with the consideration of this order we enter the wide and wonderful area of probability. Nietzsche did not know probability theory, but his philosophy points to it. An indication of his philosophical prescience is the fact that natural science is freeing itself more and more from the fetters of the causal worldview. Consideration and measure of probability are becoming increasingly important, and with these, insight into the importance of the thinker, who made his turn from metaphysical premises decades ago, should also grow.

In modern natural science, probability theory is applied to events for the same reasons for which Nietzsche fought against the mechanistic interpretation of the world. The world of the infinitely small has been discovered, which defies any predictability, any traditional categorization. All that remains are "averages." Average sizes and probabilities take the place of "exact" determination. With this, exactly what Nietzsche demanded is accomplished: the world becomes free from the compulsion of the "law." The devaluation of the concept of causation for our knowledge is the apparent expression of this process. The causal relationship between two processes is seemingly always the same, for something "repeats." The number, on the other hand, which denotes only a probable result, leaves precisely the possibility open: *that the event proceeds a little differently each time, because each time it indicates the outcome of a struggle that has just taken place.* Nature is always different – "there is no second time."

From this view, it is understandable how important Nietzsche's rejection of "causalism" is. "Two successive states, the one 'cause,' the other 'effect' — is *wrong*. The first state has no *effect*, the second has nothing *effected* in it. It is a struggle between two elements that are unequal in power: A new arrangement of forces is achieved, depending on the degree of power of each. The second state is something fundamentally different from the first (not its effect): the essential thing is that the battling factors emerge with new quanta of power."[41] The event is neither brought about nor effective, the "cause" is invented in addition to the event. The basic requirement is the belief in the return of identical cases. The interpretation of causality is thus a consequence of the categorization of the world from the point of view of consciousness. Reality knows no identical cases, but only similar ones. Categorization robs life of its character, i.e., of the *will to power*. "Every struggle — *and everything that happens is a struggle* — needs time. What we call 'cause' and 'effect' omits the struggle and therefore does not correspond to the event." In the causally determined world, identical cases seem to be subject to the same "law" in constant obedience; the real, living *happening*, on the other hand, is nothing but an incessant process of ascertaining strength. The organism should be defined as a "permanent form of processes of ascertaining strength, in which the various combatants grow unequally."[42]

The individual center of power, it was said earlier, interprets the world on its own. We can now describe this "interpretation" in more detail. The interpreter is the *will to power*. "Interpret" is just another word for a means of *being in control of something*. Mere differences in power could not perceive themselves as such. "There must be something that *wants* to grow, which interprets every other something that wants to grow in terms of its value." It is this something that wants to grow, the *will to power*, that delimits and determines degrees, that sets differences in power in the first place.[43] Due to the necessary perspectivism, each center of power constructs the rest of the world on its own — but constructing means: measuring, touching, shaping in oneself, against one's own strength.[44]

---

41   *The Will to Power*, §633.

42   *The Will to Power*, §642.

43   *The Will to Power*, §643.

44   *The Will to Power*, §636.

## 5. The Will to Power

Nothing stood in the way of understanding Nietzsche's philosophy like the title of his main philosophical work. One presumed to know what "will" and what "power" were and interpreted the title accordingly. In truth, nothing is as difficult to understand and paraphrase as what Nietzsche actually means by the term "will to power." Understanding begins at the moment when one gives up coupling the terms "will" and "goal." The *will to power* is not a will that has power as its goal, that "strives for power." The will is also not directed towards "something" — all these ideas falsify the reality of will. Insofar as purposes and goals exist, they are set by the will, they are in its service and therefore cannot be something outside of it, towards which it is "striving." Will does not strive towards any goal, it is *becoming* itself, which knows no goal. This *becoming* is *struggle*. So what is wanting? Nietzsche explains: "To want in general is as much as wanting to get *stronger*, wanting to *grow* — and wanting the means to do so."[45] Strength is not a *goal* of the will, because *it is the will itself*. The will therefore only "wants" itself: so far the declaration does not give any impetus. "Growing," however, could be understood as a passive process — then Nietzsche's image of the world would be decisively misunderstood. Growing is not a "process": Nietzsche understands *growing* to be an activity — it is nothing more than a series of victories. Nietzsche rejects causality because it conceals the world as a struggle; for the same reason, he turns against teleology: the apparent expediency in what is happening is merely the result of the *will to power*: every victory sets an order, "getting stronger brings more order, which might be misunderstood as an apparent design."[46]

The will has no external goal — it is nothing in itself: *Will* is only an expression for the overall state of being. In humans it looks like this:

---

45  *The Will to Power*, §675.

46  *The Will to Power*, §552. [This is mistakenly cited as §525 in Baeumler's text. — translator]

Willing is commanding, but commanding is a desire, and this desire is a "sudden explosion of strength." The path of the will is marked by explosive power. What we understand by "wanting" in the narrower sense, the conscious will, is only a side effect of what is essential, which is an outpouring of power. "Wanting is just a side note." The conscious will accompanies the actual will, which always has infinity before it and is therefore "free." So he is not "free" because he sets goals for himself, but the other way around — because he has no goal, because, from the point of view of consciousness, he always goes into the dark. Wanting something does not mean "striving for a goal," it means "experimenting in order to find out what we can do; only success or failure can teach us this." So all willing is in truth an ability: it is a testing of strength. This departs from the conventional doctrine of the will, and Nietzsche can say: "There is no will, neither a free nor a non-free one. Under certain circumstances, a thought is followed by an action: at the same time the *thought* arises, so does the *affect* of the commanding — to it belongs to the feeling of freedom, which one usually relocates to the 'will' itself (while it is only an accompaniment of the will)." So-called willing is a prejudice: the only fact is that something happens through us. The regularity of these events leads us to believe that what we do regularly, we "want"; so we are free. "The fact is, 'in such a case, that's what I do.' The appearance is: such and such a case has occurred — I want to do this now." If one is surprised by one's own actions, as in the case of passion, then one doubts one's freedom and one may speak of demonic influences. In such cases, our superficial psychology of will fails. The question is: what will be acted on out of pleasure, i.e., out of a feeling of abundant power, or out of displeasure, i.e., out of inhibition of the feeling of power. In no case, however, is action taken for the sake of happiness or benefit or to ward off displeasure: it "rather gives out a certain amount of force and grabs something that it can do with. That which is called a 'goal,' or 'purpose,' is in truth the means for this involuntary explosion-process."

This results in a strictly anti-hedonistic conception of the nature of real volition. Pleasure and displeasure become something secondary: they are the oldest symptoms of all value judgments, but not their causes. Above all, pleasure does not arise from the "satisfaction" of will. Since there is no "goal" of the will, there is also no end state in which the will could be satisfied. *Nothing was more hateful to Nietzsche's tense Nordic character than the oriental idea of blissful calm*, Augustine's concept of the "Sabbath of the Sabbaths." Nietzsche's doctrine of the will is the most perfect expression of his Germanism. "Happiness (*le plaisir*) as the goal of action is only a means of increasing tension: it must not be confused with the happiness that lies in the action itself. The final happiness is very definite; the happiness in the action would be denoted by a hundred such specific images of happiness." The "thereby" [*das Damit*] is an illusion: the actor mirrors a happiness that he wants to reap and forgets about the actual driving force. The goal presented is there only to increase the desire for discharge to the utmost. "There is an overflowing, charged feeling of strength: the presented goal of the action gives an anticipation of the relaxation and thereby stimulates even more primal discharge: the following action gives the actual relaxation."[47]

We say we want "something"; in truth, something wants in us. This something mirrors an image, a goal, which now acts as a motive — in truth, it is always only power that "works." All of our actions, all of our thoughts come unconnected, each for itself from the same depth of our *self*. Consciousness just watches. "Everything that comes into consciousness is the last link in a chain, a conclusion. That one thought would be the direct cause of another thought is only apparent. The actual linked events take place beneath our consciousness: the rows and

---

47  Measure the worth of Nietzschean interpretations by this decided rejection of the pleasure-displeasure principle, in which the philosopher of the *will to power* is contrasted as a Dionysian yes-man against the pessimist Schopenhauer. Nietzsche's philosophy moves beyond the pleasure-displeasure principle, and thus it also moves beyond the opposition between optimism and pessimism.

successions of feelings that appear, thoughts, etc. are *symptoms* of what is actually happening! Under every thought there is a desire. Every thought, every feeling, every will is not born from a certain instinct, but is an *overall condition*, a whole surface of the whole consciousness and results from the momentary power-situation of all of the drives that constitute us – that is, of the ruling drive, as well as those that obey or resist it. The next thought is a sign of how the entire power-situation has shifted in the meantime." Every action is something infinitely different from the "pale image of consciousness" that we have of it while it is being performed. "Purposes" are signs, nothing more. "While otherwise the copy follows the model, a kind of copy precedes the model. In truth, we never quite know what we are doing — for example, when we want to take a step or want to make a sound. Perhaps this 'want' is just a pale shadow of what is really already becoming, a subsequent reflection of our ability and doing: sometimes a very wrong one, where we seem to be unable to do what we want."

The concepts of *purpose* and *will* spoil all our reality, right down to the most mundane ideas. Everywhere we find an expediency of nature — but what we "want" and what we do are different. There is no way around it. "I eat to fill myself" — but what do I know of what satiety is! In truth, satiety is achieved, but not wanted — the momentary sensation of pleasure with every bite, as long as there is hunger, is the motive: not the intention, "to," but an attempt with every bite to see whether it still tastes good. Our actions are attempts, whether this or that impulse takes pleasure in it, right down to the most intricate, playful expressions of the urge for activity, which we misinterpret and misunderstand through the theory of purposes."

There is only a terminological, not a factual, contradiction when Nietzsche sometimes completely denies the will and then speaks of the will to power. What he denies is the conscious, goal-setting will, which belongs to the fabricated beings of the "inner world." The principle of his psychology is thus: "Sensation and thinking are sufficient here. 'Willing' as some accoutrement is an illusion." The *will to power* is not a will, but an ability; it is the actual working unit, in the place of which idealism lets consciousness work. The error of the previous philosophers was that they ascribed to the unity of consciousness what in reality the unity of power achieves, which Nietzsche calls the *will to power*. Modern anti-Cartesianism reaches its climax in the concept of the *will to power*. That is why the main work also bears this term as a title.

The "immense mistakes" of idealism can be systematically summarized as follows[48]: The fundamental error is the "nonsensical overestimation of consciousness" from which one has made a unity — a living being that feels, thinks, and wants. This being is called the "spirit." Wherever expediency, system, and coordination appear, this spirit is used as the "cause." Consciousness appears as the highest kind of being — as God. Wherever there is effect, the work of a will is assumed. The true world appears as the spiritual world and is therefore only accessible through the "facts of consciousness." Knowing is understood as an activity of consciousness. From these basic assumptions, conclusions are drawn of crucial importance. These conclusions are: All progress is in the direction of becoming conscious, becoming unconscious is regression; one approaches reality through logic, one moves away from it through the senses; the approach to the "spirit" means an approach to God; all good must come from spirituality, must be a fact of consciousness; progress towards the better can only be progress in awareness.

As Ludwig Feuerbach before him, Nietzsche sees something of Christian theology in the philosophy of the spirit from Descartes to Hegel. His criticism of consciousness and will is at the same time a critique of the Christian interpretation of the world. The idealistic worldview is just a "philosophical-moral cosmo-theodicy." It is based on the highest values and goals, which life serves — but this misunderstands the means (the "spirit") as an end, and conversely, life is degraded to

---

48   *The Will to Power*, §529.

the means. Everything is judged by the conscious world of the spirit. But the "conscious world" cannot be considered as a starting point of value: instead, an "objective value" is necessary. The mind cannot form the starting point of all our estimates because the spirit is, as a perpetrator (e.g., in our thinking), fictitious. Our thoughts are from the depths of the total unit we are. What comes into consciousness is always something derived and often something deceptive. Reality spreads to immeasurable depth under the surface of consciousness. It is not chaos, but the well-ordered realm of the *will to power*. "In terms of the monstrous multiplicity both benefiting and combatting, as is the overall life of each organism, its conscious world of feelings, intentions, and valuations is a small excerpt. This piece of consciousness as a purpose, as a *why* for the overall phenomenon of life, we are missing: It is apparent that consciousness is only a means more in the unfolding and power extension of life. Thus, it is a naiveté, desire, or spirituality, or morality, or any detail of the sphere of consciousness as the highest value: and maybe to justify the 'world' from them."[49]

The theological, moral, and hedonistic assessments and justifications of life are treated by Nietzsche as being on the same footing: they are "insane interpretations" that measure life with factors of consciousness ("pleasure and displeasure," "good and bad"). Instead of understanding consciousness as a tool and a detail in life as a whole, the relationship is reversed and a spiritual world is used as the standard for life. All real action, coming from the depths of being, appears distorted and bent with this optic: instead of fighting units of life, one believes one sees an imaginary world moving in a straight line, through spiritual values of certain units of consciousness. This is the flawed perspective from one part to the whole from which emerges the tendency of idealistic philosophers to imagine a "total consciousness," a "Spirit" or a "God." In this way the meaning shifts out of life and existence becomes the "monster," something that has to be condemned.

---

49  *The Will to Power*, §707.

"Precisely that we have eliminated the overall consciousness that sets ends and means: that is our great relief… Our greatest indictment of life was the existence of God…"[50]

From this point, Nietzsche's whole philosophical system can be surveyed. The unified basic idea of his theoretical as well as his practical philosophy becomes visible. The fight against consciousness over the subject, the will, and the spirit in the theoretical sphere corresponds to the fight against the distinction between "good" and "bad," against "guilt," the "bad conscience" and the moral "responsibility" in the practical one. Nietzsche has to fight the Christian conception of God because it nullifies the character of existence as he recognizes it: "As soon as we imagine someone is responsible for the fact that we are so and so, etc. (God, Nature), that is, our existence, our happiness and misery are ascribed to that someone, we spoil the innocence of becoming. We then have someone who wants to achieve something through us and with us."[51]

The secret of Nietzsche's struggle against the concept of God is thus revealed. A passing note in the *Nachlaß* reads: "The refutation of God: — actually only the moral God is refuted." So it is only the *priestly* concept of God against which the fight is directed — the God of the *priest* is dead. Only a God can live in our hearts who leaves existence, eternal becoming, its innocence. As if in hard stone, Nietzsche chisels the words that paraphrase his religion of fate: "Nobody is responsible for the fact that he is there at all, that he is made in such a way, that he exists under these circumstances, in this environment. The fatality of his essence cannot be detached from the fatality of everything that was and will be. It is not the result of an intention, a will, an end; an attempt is not made with it, an 'ideal of man' or an 'ideal of happiness' or to achieve an 'ideal of morality' — it is absurd to want to shift one's being

---

50  *The Will to Power*, §707.

51  *The Will to Power*, §552.

to some purpose."[52] There is no such thing as a "criticism of being," because this would presuppose that we have a fixed point outside of being from which we can assess it. But in every assessment of self this being still exists — whether we say *yes* or *no* to existence — we always only do what we are. All valuations are only consequences and perspectives in service of the *will to power*.[53] *Will to power* is just another term for the *innocence of becoming*.

From this central concept Nietzsche explains his own *will to philosophy* and the ways of this will – he interprets himself with the help of a basic concept of his system: "How long has it been now since I tried to prove the perfect innocence of becoming! And what strange paths I have already taken! Once this seemed to me the correct solution: that I decreed: 'Being is as something of a work of art, not at all under the *jurisdictio* of morality; rather, morality belongs itself to the realm of appearance.' Another time I said: 'All concepts of guilt are objective and completely worthless, but subjective, all life is *necessarily* unjust and alogical.' A third time I won the *denial* of all purposes and felt that the causal connections were unrecognizable. And why is all this? Wasn't it to create the feeling of complete irresponsibility for myself — to position myself outside of any praise and blame, independent of all past and present, in order to pursue my goal in my own way?"

When Nietzsche first began *The Will to Power*, which would be his actual philosophical work and for which *Zarathustra* was only the "vestibule," he wrote down the title, among other things: "The Innocence of Becoming: A Guide to the Redemption of Morality." This title has been supplanted by a more active, more charged one. However, there is nothing better suited to understanding what is philosophically important than that first draft of the title, which can hardly be misunderstood. This title means: as soon as we set a being independent and above becoming, reality is deprived of its meaning.

---

52   *Twilight of the Idols*, "The Four Great Errors."

53   *The Will to Power*, §675.

It becomes an "apparent" world alongside the real one — it becomes *superfluous*. The hypothesis of a "true" being is therefore in the service of world slander. In truth, becoming is "of equal value in every moment … in other words: it has no value at all, because something is missing by which it can be measured."[54] There is no counterpart to life from which one can reflect on existence, there is no authority before which life could be ashamed: this is the innocence of becoming. Life has no judge: "one has to see the absurdity of this gesture that establishes existence."[55] Establishing what *is* seems to the realist to be something unspeakably higher and more serious than any "ought to be."[56] "A person as he *ought to be*: that sounds as absurd to us as: 'A tree as it ought to be.'"[57] Morality contains nothing but desires — but just when people dream up ideals, they become small. "You cannot have respect for a man — when you see how he gets by, endures, how he expoits circumstances or pummels opponents; if, however, you see him in light of his desires, he is the most absurd beast…"[58] There is something *feminine* in all desires: it is as if man "needed a playground of cowardice, laziness, weakness, sweetness, submissiveness to recuperate from his strong and masculine virtues."[59]

From a philosophical point of view, that the concept of "innocence" excludes the means by which one arrives at a goal is particularly noteworthy. Part of the innocence of existence is its presence: "the present must never be justified for the sake of a future or the past for the sake of the present." Therefore it is necessary "to deny an overall consciousness of becoming, of a 'God,' in order not to consider events from the

---

54  *The Will to Power*, §708.

55  *The Will to Power*, §675.

56  *The Will to Power*, §333.

57  *The Will to Power*, §332.

58  *The Will to Power*, §335.

59  Ibid.

point of view of a sympathetic, knowing and yet *unwilling* being."[60] But once such a being has been imagined, the logic of things then disproves the belief in the "true" world behind the real one, the belief in morality, the highest values and purposes of life itself, and a state is reached in which that fundamental error manifests itself everywhere like a sickness introduced into a healthy body — then we are faced with the phenomenon of Nihilism. Nietzsche's planned main work[61] begins with a description of such Nihilism. *Nihilism* means that the highest values are devalued; Nihilism is the logic of our ideals that has been thought through to the end.

It is usually thought that Nietzsche did nothing more than register the fact of European Nihilism, that he was essentially a critic, a mere annihilator and destroyer who left rebuilding to others. This accusatory position is in line with his supposed cheap statements of "atheism." Nietzsche sees Nihilism as the foundation of modern culture and has ruthlessly exposed the chaos of the modern soul; but he has also established a new, purer picture of the world with man standing upright. Its meaning does not consist in the fact that he has done what so many before him did — he also had weary hours — : that he formulated "new" values, "new" ideals, but rather in the fact that he showed us the depths of reality more than any thinker before him. He did not coldly and impotently describe the world of rubble that surrounds people who were brought up by idealism, but he also showed the world order that was and always will be. This demonstration of the eternal world order, which constitutes his actual philosophical achievement, is closely related to his belief in fate. He only destroyed the wrong order of consciousness in order to allow the true order of the *will to power* to take its place in our thoughts, just as he declared the feud with the moral god without fighting God.

---

60   *The Will to Power*, §708.

61   That is, *The Will to Power*. [trans.]

## 6. The Heraclitic World

Philosophy, which begins with the subject, the "facts of consciousness," ends with the assumption of a total consciousness or a world of spiritual values. Nietzsche's philosophy of "objective valuation" culminates in the statement that there is an "overall phenomenon of life," a unity of life from which all of our thoughts and actions emerge. The *will to power* is just another name for this unity. By this will, we do not have to understand a subjective phenomenon, an exertion of the will or an impulse of will, but something objective: it is well-being as the reality of life. The unity of the organism and the totality of life, indeed of existence in general, are regarded by Nietzsche as having the same essence. The difference in size that exists between the human body and the cosmos does not matter if in both cases we consider the structure that follows from the fundamental nature of the *will to power*, because both — body and cosmos — are infinitely articulated multitudes, constituted by the *will to power*. "When analyzed in depth, whether our body or the universe, the lines between organic and inorganic are no longer apparent."[62]

The "soul" from which the "subject" of the idealists ultimately emerged may have been an attractive and mysterious thought — but perhaps, says Nietzsche, what we are now learning to exchange for it is even more attractive and mysterious.[63] "The human body, in which the whole of the most distant and immediate past of all organic becoming comes alive and manifests again, through which an enormous, inaudible current seems to flow: the body is a more astonishing thought

---

62  *The Will to Power*, §676.

63  *The Will to Power*, §659. The words of Novalis, which mean the opposite, sound similar: "The outside is only an inside raised in a state of secrecy." Novalis starts from the inside — the outside is only a symbol to him. His thought therefore presupposes that the inside is closer to us than the outside. Nietzsche thinks the other way around. Nietzsche is not a Romantic. Bringing him into this context means for him to contest his fate in the history of Europe and to rob his philosophy of meaning.

than the old 'soul.'" "On the guide of the body" he wanders through the realms of Nature and history. The living body is the most perfect manifestation of the *will to power*; it is the phenomenon in which we find all traits of this will most clearly expressed. Nietzsche's philosophy is a singular hymn of praise to the reality of the living body. It is the philosophy of a genuinely Hellenic instinct.

But what is the living body? It is a political entity — an *aristocracy*.[64] The *will to power* is not expressed in subjective ideas and moods, not in accidental wills and desires, but in the "structure of domination" that we call the living body. "The greater complexity, the sharp distinction, the juxtaposition of the developed organs and functions, with the disappearance of the middle limbs — if *that* is *perfection*, then there is a will to power in the organic process; by virtue of its dominating, formative, commanding powers, it is always increasing and simplifying its sphere of power: it grows imperatively."[65] We saw that life is to be defined as a "permanent form" of processes of ascertaining strength, in which the various fighters themselves grow unequally. Nietzsche continues this explanation in such a way that the political character of the organism becomes completely clear: "To what extent there is a reluctance to obey; individual power is by no means given up. Likewise, in commanding there is an admission that the absolute power of the opponent is not defeated, incorporated, or dissolved. 'Obeying' and 'commanding' are forms of the fighting game."[66]

The struggle to which the philosophy of the *will to power* traces everything is therefore not a senseless raging of forces against each other. There is an order in it, and the thoughts of this order must be understood if one wants to understand Nietzsche's philosophy.

Once again, the incompleteness of the system-building is palpable. But there are pieces in the *Nachlaß* that we can use to close this gap. In

---

64  *The Will to Power*, §660.

65  *The Will to Power*, §644.

66  *The Will to Power*, §642.

organic beings, says one note, it is not an individual being who wants to maintain a subject, but the *struggle itself* wants to maintain itself, wants to grow and become conscious. "What we call 'consciousness' and 'spirit' is only a means and a tool, by virtue of which — not a *subject* — but a *struggle* wants to maintain itself. Man is the testimony to which tremendous forces can be set in motion by a small being of manifold content (or through a perennial fight, concentrated on many small beings) — beings who play with stars..." So there is something else besides the fight: it is what makes the fight "perennial," what the "permanent form" of the living makes possible, what builds the "structure of domination" of the body, what prevents those who fight from being destroyed. This cannot be anything that lies outside of the struggle — this prerequisite does not fit a system that wants to represent becoming "from within." It cannot be a "law" that prescribes rules for the struggle — it can only be the equilibrium that is established *in* and *through* struggle, and thus maintains the struggle. "The struggle as the means of equilibrium" is indeed one of the notes. The context of the "will to power" demands that this sentence keep its meaning even when reversed: equilibrium is a means of struggle.

I am convinced that the philosophy of *The Will to Power* culminates in the cited sentences and their reversal. If we read elsewhere that a position of equilibrium has never been reached, it proves that it is not possible,[67] that is no objection. Because the "position of equilibrium" here means *standstill* ("If standstill were possible, it would have occurred") — the word "equilibrium" has a purely mechanical meaning here. In contrast, the principle of struggle as a means of equilibrium has a metaphysical meaning. In order to make this sense clear, it must be said what Nietzsche means by *struggle*.

Nothing impedes understanding Nietzsche's philosophical system with such stubbornness as the prejudice, born of a poor interpretation

---

67  *The Will to Power*, §1064.

of his writings, that he had "changed" several times.[68] In truth there are few thinkers in the whole history of philosophy who followed a single thought from youth with such certainty as Nietzsche. One must not be fooled by his variety of expressions; in the following section this completely puzzling change of "attitudes" will be explained: Nietzsche's writings are the works of a fencer; each individual work is to be understood from a particular fencing position. *Behind the change of position, the basic concept of the Heraclitic world remains unchanged.* Just as it opened up to the young man, so the man represented it in the "will to power" with the developed forces of his whole being. The agreement is so perfect that we can even use sentences about Heraclitus from the fragment on *Philosophy in the Tragic Age of the Greeks*[69] to interpret the *will to power*.

With a truly wonderful decisiveness, the young Nietzsche knew how to keep himself free from the moral ideas of his time. From the beginning, he had access to a world that lay before him in pure clarity, untouched by the lying and flimsy concepts of bourgeois humanity. The youth sees a thunderstorm. Then he wrote to a friend: "What were the eternal 'Thou shalt', 'Thou shalt not'! How different the lightning, storm, and hail: free powers without ethics!"[70] Not the act of the eternal symbols: the pleasure of fighting and winning, the uninhibited view of the world's character as an eternal struggle of forces is what alienates him from bourgeois morality. Far more directly and deeply than the mystical-musical, youthful work on tragedy, the small fragment on Homer's competition introduces his idea of life. The competition is for him the "noblest Hellenic foundational idea." The Greek genius, he recognizes, accepted the good Eris[71] – nothing separates the Greek

---

68   For examples of this "prejudiced" perspective, see the Nietzsche-related writings of Karl Jaspers, Karl Löwith, and Walter Kaufmann. [trans.]

69   This is Nietzsche's incomplete book (1873) on the philosophy of Thales, Anaximander, Heraclitus, Parmenides, and Anaxagoras. [trans.]

70   To Carl von Gersdorff, 07 April 1866.

71   Eris is the Greek goddess of strife and discord. [trans.]

world so much from ours. How barbaric, how unfathomable in the deepest depths — but how true it is when he defines in that fragment: "The cruelty of victory is the pinnacle of life's happiness." One does not understand Nietzsche's life and writings if one does not consider what value the experience and the concept of struggle and victory have for him. In the later preface to the writing that detached him from Wagner (*Human, All Too Human*), the most significant event of his life shines before us as an event of victory: "an enigmatic, questionable victory, but the first victory after all ..." In the preface to *The Joyful Wisdom*, every philosophy that places peace above war is interpreted as a *symptom of disease*. And in *Twilight of the Idols* ("Morality as Anti-Nature") it says: "You have renounced the great life if you renounce the war..."

In bourgeois-humanitarian society, the struggle is treated as something that *not ought to be*, at best as something to be excused. In this society, love is prized — a feeling, a state of mind, something subjective in any case, and above all something ambiguous, which can be understood as *eros*, *sexus*, or also as divine love. Nothing reflects the indeterminacy — i.e., the "inwardness" — of the bourgeois personality better than this protean concept. Where *amor* and *caritas*[72] shake hands in the shadow of the banks — that is where this society is located.

A single word by the young Nietzsche glaringly illuminates the historical relativity of this world, theoretically constituted by "love," practically by the lie: "*Envy* is much more pronounced among the Greeks. The concept of *justice* is much more important to them than it is for us: Christianity knows no justice." What does that word mean? Nietzsche must be completely at home in the depths of another cosmos in order to be able to express it at all. The Christian God is presented as the just judge, the Christian life is limited by an act of divine jurisdiction, the last day.

*Iudex ergo cum sedebit,*

---

72  "... *amor* and *caritas* ..." — i.e., love and the Christian love of humankind... [trans.]

*Quidquid latet apparebit,*

*Nil inultum remanebit.*[73]

How did Nietzsche come to deny Christianity's justice? *Because he lives entirely in the Heraclitic conception of justice.* In the deepest depths, the idea of a rewarding and punishing justice is foreign and incomprehensible to him — indeed the idea of the court in general, whereby there is a morally accused, an enthroned judge and an objective verdict is alien to him. This juridical way of thinking only prepares the way for a judgment according to the points of view "good" and "bad." It belongs to a kind of person who is not active, who only reacts. The reacting person, the person of resentment, ultimately derives demands on others from "justice." But being fair is always positive behavior: "The active, the attacking, aggressive person is still one hundred steps closer to justice than the reactive."[74] The attacking person is closer to justice than the reactive one because *justice can be anything, only not what the reactive person would like it to be*: a means of abolishing the struggle to balance the opposites, to achieve peace. A legal system that would not be "a means in the struggle of power complexes," but a means against all struggle in general, is what Nietzsche calls *a hostile principle, a destroyer and dissolver of people, a sign of fatigue, a secret path to nothing.*[75] It is morality that teaches us to take this bypass, the morality of the "good and just," who are the *greatest danger* to all human futures.[76]

---

73  *The judge so sits*
    *Whatever lies hidden will appear*
    *Nothing will go unpunished.* [From the Latin poem "Day of Wrath" (*Dies irae*) — trans.]

74  *Genealogy of Morals*, II, §11.

75  *Genealogy of Morals*, II, §11.

76  *Zarathustra*, "On the Old and New Tables," §27. ["Where the strong are weak, where the noble are all-too-gentle – there buildeth it its loathsome nest; the parasite liveth where the great have small sore-places…. The *good* — they have always been the beginning of the end…. With whom lieth the greatest danger to the whole human future? Is it not with the *good* and *just*? … False shores

Justice finally becomes the virtue of the last people: "And when they say: 'I am just,' it always sounds the same as: 'I am avenged'!"[77] The vengeful person, the person of resentment , wants all men to be equal, but Zarathustra teaches: "For men are not equal: thus speaks justice."[78]

Inequality and struggle are the prerequisites for justice. This justice does not rule over the world, nor over the crowd of those who quarrel, it knows no guilt and no responsibility, no judicial process and no verdict: it is immanent in the struggle. That is why it is not possible in a world of peace. Justice can only exist where forces are measured against each other in *freedom*. Under an absolute authority, in an order of things that a divine Lord knows, in the realm of the *Pax Romana*, there is no longer any justice, because there is no longer any struggle. Then the world freezes in a conventional form. Nietzsche, on the other hand, sees that out of the struggle itself justice is born anew at every moment; the struggle is the father of all things, it makes the master *master* and the slave *slave*. Thus spoke Heraclitus of Ephesus. But this is also the primordial Germanic view: *in battle it becomes apparent who is noble and who is not*; by innate courage the master becomes master, and by cowardice the slave becomes slave. It is precisely in this that eternal justice expresses itself: it organizes and divides, it creates the order of the world, it is the author of every rank. Nietzsche's great teaching arises from the core idea of the Greco-Germanic metaphysics: there is no such thing as *Morality*, but only a morality for masters and a morality for slaves.[79]

Justice is not established through a forensic act, i.e., outwardly, but rather through the deed itself. If Schopenhauer's main work bears the

---

and false securities did the good teach you; in the lies of the good were ye born and bred. Everything hath been radically contorted and distorted by the *good*." Thomas Common's translation, from multiple sections within "On the Old and New Tables" — trans.]

77  *Zarathustra*, "On the Virtuous."

78  *Zarathustra*, "On the Scholars."

79  *Beyond Good and Evil*, §260.

title: *The World as Will and Idea*, Nietzsche's work could bear the title: *The World as Deed and Justice* or, more briefly, expressing the same thing: *The World as Struggle*. This latter is just another twist on the innocence of becoming. The "innocence" consists in the fact that there is no "perpetrator" in everything that is done, but *that* something happens, that there is no "subject," no purposes and no causal connections. "Perpetrator" means something like *responsible perpetrator*. The real act is not excluded, because the real perpetrator is a fighter, a quantum of power that draws all the consequences from his strength at every moment. A center of power is not a responsible "subject." The decisive factor is the exclusion of consciousness and responsibility: all the lines of Nietzsche's philosophy intersect in this thought. From it follows the non-forensic consideration of human existence. There is only a judge of life if there is a "spirit." The spirit not only faces life, but it is above it, and it is precisely through this that the innocence of the struggle is abolished. The fight is no longer decided by those who fight, but by some otherworldly power, for which it is not the strength but the "good conscience" that is decisive. When consciousness falls, so does the idea of responsibility and judgment — life regains its innocence.

Nietzsche's warlike nature is not only expressed in his polemical writings, in his agonal relationship to Schopenhauer, Wagner, and Bismarck, in the daring courage with which he attacks the oldest and most revered; rather, his warrior nature also determines the character of all his thoughts. The exclusion of the *forensic* system is a necessary consequence of the fact that Nietzsche is a warrior down to his instincts. Because it is warlike to always live in the face of "another," to always feel that you are in tension with certain forces. *Force against force* — that is the character of life. On the other hand, it is priestly to measure and judge life from an absolute standpoint above life. The priest appeals to God, and with that he is released from battle. In virtue of the special relationship he has claimed with God, he is right without having won. *The type of the priest thus contrasts with that of the fighter.* It is no coincidence that peoples like the Germans and the Greeks do not know priests in the sense of the Mediterranean cultures. When the priest takes up his sword, he does not become a warrior, but a fighter for faith, a defender of the highest God, a fanatic. He fights for the absolute, which wins in every case; if it does not win through him now, it will win later. It is clear that with such an appeal to the Absolute, the conception of justice or fate is impossible. For the warrior there is no absolute; he only knows his own strength and fate. The priestly and warrior systems are mutually exclusive.

All his life Nietzsche was at war with two historical worlds: against the *priestly*-Romantic and against the *rational*-Enlightenment. His Heraklitic system gives us information about the profound necessity of the alignment of these fronts. *The world of the priest and the world of the enlightener have in common that real struggle and justice do not occur in them.* The priest judges and then wages wars of extermination in order to execute the judgment he declared "divine." How different does the world of the Enlightenment appear on the other hand — and yet here, too, an absolute is revered. Instead of kneeling before the saint, there is the self-conscious kipper before reason. In both worlds is the free struggle of forces with the *great spell* set. Forces and their opposites are not recognized at all by the Enlightenment. It only knows rational beings with feeling and taste, subjects whose judgments can be corrected and formed. Everything else is "raw" nature. Its highest concept is a harmony that excludes serious contradiction, real struggle. In place of the struggle of forces, there is the rational and moral struggle of enlightened spirits against superstition, stupidity, and malice of men. This is no longer a fight in the sense of the born warrior: how could you fight if you are right from the start! How could one fight in a world in which there is no struggle, in which there are only *degrees* of understanding, enlightenment, and education! Each force has its perspective and it fights within that perspective. So there is no struggle for reason, for happiness, for progress. Victory has already been achieved — the good is on one side, and only evil on the other. In this respect *the enlightener is a secularized priest*: like the priest in his light of God, so the enlightener stands in the light of reason.

But the enlightener thinks he is higher than the priest, and he even surpasses the priest in orthodoxy. This is because the enlightener has one thing on the priest: the idea of *tolerance*. In his fanaticism the priest is great; he can become a hero in contradiction to his teaching. That is why Zarathustra passes the priests by. Only the religious fighters spoil the honest fighting game with their faith; they know nothing about justice. The enlighteners, however, kill justice with subtle poisons. *The idea of tolerance is the contradiction of justice*: it abolishes the contradiction, it confuses the order of things, because it names the struggle as something that is to be condemned. The priest invented the guilty conscience and morality in order to conquer and rule; he fights against the unbelievers because he thinks he is in grace his opposites dwell in damnation. The enlightener pretends to no longer fight, to no longer want to win and rule; he only serves morality. He is too enlightened to build immolation stakes, he is setting up "chairs of virtue." He is content with having a good conscience for himself and teaching that his opponents do not have it. This is what he calls tolerance: *the denial of opposites so that he can rule without the trouble of fighting*. And that is his philosophy: all living and powerful things are traced back to tendencies of consciousness, to "reason" and "will." In doing so, he makes the big things small and the small big. The priest fights for the cause of God. But when the enlightened citizen wages war, he has to invent a "good cause" that is worth fighting for, because he — of course — only fights with a clear conscience. "You say that it is the good thing that sanctifies war? I tell you: it is the good war that sanctifies every thing."[80] But the moralism of the Enlightenment must end with the complete rejection of war. The unheroic existence, the life without great goals, the "pitiful comfort" is presented as a moral duty; the war that unleashes heroism is ostracized.

---

80  *Zarathustra*, "On War and Warriors."

Modern history has two epochs: the epoch of priestly values is followed by the epoch of moral values. Nietzsche's psychology of the priest (of resentment) in the *Genealogy* is the continuation of the struggle against morality initiated in *The Dawn*. Solemnly, the attention of the priest strains, the servants of the holy and the servants of reason are of the same kind: *they revolt in the name of the absolute, they condemn, they ostracize instead of fighting*. At the same time, however, they master human, all-too-human means to achieve their ends. In order to achieve victory, morality must become immoral. "For moral values to prevail, immoral forces and passions must help them."[81] The enlightener endures this contradiction. *He lacks the honesty and bravery that go with fighting a contradicting state of affairs*. The enlightener endures it in the midst of the lies of Christian civilization; he still has a good conscience even in the lie. But that is the psychological formula for anarchy. The order based on the rule of consciousness is only an apparent one: it is not based on the essence of things; it contradicts reality. When people believe in a fictitious harmony, in a world without forces and opposites, then chaos occurs. Nature is not chaotic — it is the realm of strict justice. The world of people becomes chaotic when they seek to emancipate themselves from the justice that lies in the essence of things, when they deny the *will to power*. Nihilism, chaos — these are the necessary consequences of the belief in harmony without struggle, in an order without contradictions. The true order arises from the relations of domination that the *will to power* produces. *Human*, we add, is a world in which *hierarchy* applies, not a world in which moral concepts speak. Inhuman is only chaos. The rule of tolerance and moral ideas, reason and compassion, in short "humanitarianism," leads to inhumanity.

If one wants to get an idea of the unity and consistency of Nietzschean thought, one must read the section on Heraclitus and the concept of justice in *Philosophy in the Tragic Age of the Greeks*. Surrounded by

---

81   *The Will to Power*, §266.

quotes from Schopenhauer's main work, which have no inner relation-ship to the communicated vision, the basic idea of *The Will To Power* can be found here in wonderful clarity. Eternal and sole *becoming*, the complete impermanence of everything real, is called a "terrible and numbing idea." Heraclitus has understood that all opposing qualities in the world are attached to one another "like two wrestlers," of whom now one, now the other, gains supremacy. The world is a mixing jug that must be constantly stirred. "All becoming arises from the war of opposites: the specific and constantly appearing qualities only express the momentary preponderance of the one fighter..." And yet there is something constant in the eternal quarrel — the mixing jug is being stirred "constantly." The mere argument would cancel itself out. To Heraclitus, the Hellenic, this quarrel reveals eternal justice.

> It is a wonderful idea, drawn from the purest borne of the Hellenic, which regards strife as the continuous rule, and strict justice bound by eternal laws. Only a Greek was able to mark this idea as the foundation of a cos-modicy; Hesiod's Good Eris is transfigured into a world principle, the idea of competition between the individual Greeks and the Greek state, from the gymnasia and palaces, from the artistic struggle, from the struggle of the political parties and the cities with one another, is transferred into the most general, so that now every Greek struggles as if he were the only one in the right, and an infinitely certain measure of judicial judgment determines at every moment in which direction the victory is headed; so the qualities wrestle with one another, for unbreakable, that immanent fight between laws and masses. The things themselves, in the standing and withstanding of which the narrow human and animal believes, have no real existence at all; they are the flashes of lightning and the flash of sparks from drawn swords, they are the gleam of victory in the battle of opposing qualities.

All of Nietzsche's decisive positions: he rejects subjective philosophy, teleology, and the concept of causation; he struggles against optimism, moralism, and progress. *The Will to Power* is anticipated here, and the concept of *justice* is revealed as its deepest concept. Where did this term go later? Why does *The Will to Power* not include a section on justice?

Justice plays an important role in the young Nietzsche's thought. It not only appears as the main concept in the description of the Aeschylean tragedy,[82] but also forms the ideal focus of the two most important *Untimely Meditations*. In the second "untimely meditation," one who has the instinct and the "power to justness" is called the most venerable specimen of the human species. Justice is contrasted with objectivity: "Objectivity and justice have nothing to do with each other."[83] Objectivity is to be understood as the "cold and contemptuous neutrality of the so-called scientific man."[84] The power of justice enables people to overcome the "common empirical truth" in recognizing history through a deeper and more just view of things. The historical world does not open up to scientific curiosity and objectivity: the past can only be interpreted from the highest power of the present. Justice does not include acceptance and tolerance, but strength and size.

If we follow the waves that give us the *Untimely Meditations* with their decisive combination of the concepts of justice and knowledge, then we get an answer to the most difficult question that exists in Nietzsche's philosophy: the question of the possibility of knowledge. In relation to the problem of knowledge, the philosophy of *The Will to Power* is in a dangerous position. Here idealism has its strongest position; here all relativism is doomed to failure. A metaphysics of justice, of course, could not be relativistic; justice excludes relativism. So the question has to be: is there a connection between this concept and the philosophy of the *will to power*.

According to the doctrine of the *will to power*, all human doing and thinking can be traced back to instincts. Even the will to truth can only be an impulse to power: the greater part of conscious thinking,

---

82  *The Birth of Tragedy*, §9.

83  "On the Advantages and Disadvantages of History," §6.

84  "Schopenhauer as Educator," §4.

even philosophical thinking, belongs to instinctive activities.[85] How could an "egotistical" drive to power be brought into connection with pure knowledge? But there is no such thing as pure knowledge if it is understood to mean the knowledge of an "uninvolved," cold, objectively observing subject — for there is such a subject. Knowledge must be relative to the knower. But since the knower is a power-quantum, the knowledge must have a relation to the power of the knower. All thinking is a form of the will to rule; every instinct that makes use of consciousness to think wants to "go somewhere." In the long history of *homo sapiens*, all basic human instincts have "already practiced philosophy." Every single one would like to represent himself as the ultimate purpose of existence and as the "justified master" of all other instincts. "Because every instinct is domineering: and as such it tries to philosophize."[86]

If one understands the world of the *will to power* as a chaos of wildly thriving forces, then knowledge is impossible. The world Nietzsche saw, however, has an eternal order within: the weaker can only be overcome by the mightier, there is no arbitrariness; The formula of the *will to power* is the formula of a law — of course a different "law" than was previously known. It does not signify a "law" over things, not something general, something beyond, against which everything in this world is exhausted as a mere "instance," but the law is in the things themselves, in their victory and defeat, in the way how they put themselves in relation to one another. It is nothing other than the alternating constant relationship between the forces of conflict themselves. This relationship, this equilibrium, is what Heraclitus understood by eternal justice.

Nietzsche's epistemology follows from this concept of justice. The transcendent concept of the "law" corresponds to a transcendent subject of knowledge who is neutral, uninvolved, "disinterested" and

---

85   *Beyond Good and Evil*, §3.

86   *Beyond Good and Evil*, §6.

is therefore called *pure*. From the immanent concept of the law, on the other hand, it follows that every instinct, every organizing center of power is only able to penetrate with its knowledge as far as its *will to power* reaches. Only insofar as and so strongly that an individual participates in the struggle can he discern. This struggle is waged with all means – also with the help of consciousness. In the frenzy of victory, Nietzsche gave too little to this means. But his basic view remains: what *knows*, what *philosophizes* is the *will to power* and not consciousness. It depends on the pathos, it depends on the strength of the thinker how far he gets in cognition. He who has the most frenzied [*weitesten gespannten*] will, the highest power, also has the highest justice, and he comes closest to the truth. For justice only abides where there is power. There is no justice without power — but neither is there true power without justice.

Only the superior, only the dominant, is able to establish "justice," i.e., to establish a standard by which it is measured; and the more powerful he is, the further he can go in "letting go." So we read in a note from the time of the *The Will to Power*. And also: "Justice, as a function of a far-sighted power that looks beyond the small perspectives of good and evil — that is, has a wider horizon of advantage…" So there is a necessary relationship between justice and power. But what can the highest power be but the power of the whole? *Justice* is just another word for the existence of this whole, for the self-preservation of this whole, which in order to be *power* for all eternity, maintains itself in equilibrium for all eternity, and which is only maintained in equilibrium in order to affirm one another in the struggle of all qualities for all eternity. The *will to power* is just another expression for the *highest justice*. Man does not know because he has consciousness — consciousness is only a means; but he knows, that is, he has a relationship to the whole, because in him the *will to power* reaches the highest point among all beings, because it is closest to eternal justice.

That we are on the right path with our interpretation is shown by a brief note of incredible impact: "Justice as a constructive, eliminating, destructive way of thinking, based on the values: the highest representative of life itself."

If *justice* can be called the "highest representative of life itself," then the definition of *truth*, which corresponds to the philosophy of the will, is: Truth is the highest representative of life itself.[87]

## 7. Dionysus. The Eternal Return

The philosophy of the *will to power*, the philosophy of eternal becoming, passes at its peak into the concept of being. Becoming *is*. This is not a being next to or above becoming — this "being" is rather only an expression of duration, self-preservation, the immanent order, the justice of *becoming* itself.

Nietzsche was very much concerned with the problem of the transition from becoming to being. One of the most famous parts of his philosophy is the doctrine of the Eternal Return, which objectively is nothing but an attempt to void the image of eternal becoming and replace it with an image of eternal being. Here, too, the *will to power* is decisive — only it does not appear as immanent power, as the highest justice, but as the act of an individual: Zarathustra. "To stamp the character of being onto becoming – that is the highest will to power... That everything recurs is the most extreme approximation of a world of becoming to that of being: — the summit of contemplation."[88]

---

87  Ernst Bertram's *Nietzsche: An Attempt at a Mythology* (1918) shows what an interpretation of Nietzsche looks like that does not start from the *will to power*. Bertram dedicates a section to the concept of justice, which opens with a word from Bishop Bossuet and which is intended to provide new evidence for Nietzsche's "thinking that always crucifies itself anew." The basic Greek character of his philosophy is completely misunderstood, his plastic concept of justice is twisted into a Christian-dialectical non-concept. He should speak of a "justice of the unjust," of a kind of "theodicy of evil," and even Nietzsche's attitude towards his own "suffering for life" should be reflected in it.

88  *The Will to Power*, §617.

In these sentences the idea of the Eternal Return appears connected with the fundamental idea of the system. Or more correctly: the thought of the Eternal Return seems to undo the system. When the concept of the Eternal Return appears, the Heraclitic character of the world disappears: "I teach you salvation from the eternal river: the river always flows back into itself, and again and again you rise into the same river as the same one." Obviously, we are faced with a contradiction here. Only one thing can apply: either the doctrine of the Eternal Return or the doctrine of the *will to power*.

The idea of the Eternal Return originates with a shock Nietzsche had while recovering in the solitude of the Engadin in August 1881. The thought is introduced at the end of *The Joyful Wisdom*[89]; it is proclaimed by Zarathustra. It is not surprising it attracted particular attention and that one was inclined to assume that the philosophical depth and significance of this thought must be in proportion to the forcefulness with which it is presented. In truth, this thought is irrelevant from the perspective of Nietzsche's system. We have to regard it as the expression of a highly personal experience. It has no connection with the basic idea of *The Will to Power*; indeed, if it were adopted, it would break the context of the philosophy of *The Will To Power*. Relation to the *will to power* is only externally established in the cited sentences: the character of being is stamped on becoming by an individual. It arises from the action of a subject. The *will to power*, however, is not a designation for an experience or event, but a formula for what happens in general. This formula has an objective meaning — hence its internal relation to the concept of justice. Through the thought of the Eternal Return everything is turned into the subjective. Nietzsche himself, as a unique person, appears at the center of world events, similar to the founder of a religion: for mankind, it is always the hour of the "great noon" in which this thought occurs. It is less a question of the value of the thought itself than of the effect it is supposed to have

---

89 See §341. [trans.]

on humanity. It marks a turning point in history: *those who do not believe in it must die out.* "Only those who consider their existence to be eternally repeatable are left: but among them a condition is possible that no utopian has yet reached." Whoever incorporates this "thought of thoughts" will be transformed. "The question in everything I do: would I wish to do it countless times? This is the greatest weight."

This is what Nietzsche tried to express objectively through the thought of the Eternal Return: the innocence and aimlessness of existence, the justification of life by itself, is expressed much more perfectly through his system. It must be remembered that the concept originates from a time when Nietzsche was still developing the idea of the *will to power.* The thought of the Eternal Return is germinated with the Zarathustra-idea; however, it was not Nietzsche's intent to always want to *remain* Zarathustra. *Zarathustra* was merely a call that was to bring him companions. The insertion of the Zarathustra-idea into the later system is perhaps only due to the fact that this call went unheard. A factual insertion of the idea of the Eternal Return into Nietzsche's later system is not possible: the Eternal Return is a religious concept, while this one, on the other hand, is a strictly philosophical one; with the former, the question of truth cannot be asked; here, on the other hand, it *must* be asked; there,[90] everything depends on the possible effect; here,[91] it is a question of the immanent depth of a new picture of the world.

The fundamental religious character of the Eternal Return is clear and Nietzsche has emphasized it. "Let's press the image of eternity on our lives! This thought embodies more than all religions that despised this life as fleeting and taught us to look towards an afterlife." The *Great Noon* is a religious vision, and Nietzsche appears to us like a redeemer: "I teach you the salvation of the eternal river…" He has accused Plato of *Egyptianism*: Plato dehistoricized the world by considering it *sub specie*

---

90  That is, with the *Eternal Return.* [trans.]

91  That is, with the *will to power.* [trans.]

*aeterni*. An Egyptization of the Heraclitic world transforms Nietzsche into a religious founder. There is nothing in his philosophical system with which this alienation of the future could be connected — the thought of the Eternal Return in *The Will to Power* stands lonely, an erratic block. There is no *philosophy* of the Eternal Return; there is only a *religion* of the Eternal Return. When Nietzsche gave in to Surlej's inspiration, he was for a moment inferior to the god-building instinct. The surest sign that we are no longer dealing with the philosopher Nietzsche is the "*Yea* and *Amen* Song," referring to the Eternal Return, with which the third part of the *Zarathustra* closes, and with his emphasis on the concept of *love* ("For I love thee, O Eternity!"). Nietzsche stands in contrast to all philosophical positions.

Drafts for *The Will to Power* show that Nietzsche wanted to rename the last chapter, "Eternal Return," to "Dionysus: Philosophy of the Eternal Return." There are also drafts in which this last book does not contain *any* reference to the Eternal Return. "The Great War," too, is sometimes called "the struggle between false and true values." The publishers of *The Will to Power* have placed an aphorism at the work's end which contains the most intimate connection of the terms *Dionysian world*, *Eternal Return* and *will to power*. It is that prose masterpiece that begins with the words: "And do you also know what 'the world' is to me? Shall I show it to you in my mirror?"[92] The consequence of my thought is the proof this fragment does not offer the ideal formula for Nietzsche's philosophical world view, as one had to assume up to now that one rather has only the choice either to regard the *will to power* as the actual system of Nietzsche, or to discard this system and explain the Dionysian aspect of Nietzsche's actual philosophy.

The only concept that is common to the aforementioned aphorism and Nietzsche's system is that of *force* [*Kraft*]. The world is described here as a "play of forces and waves of force," as a "sea of storming and flowing forces within itself," as something that changes and that always

---

92  *The Will to Power*, §1067. [trans.]

recedes into itself. The Eternal Return is interpreted as a symbol of the self-affirmation of this power. It gives eternal becoming the character of a movement "which knows no satiety, no weariness, no fatigue." It gives it the character of happiness, the symbol of which is the *circle*. On the other hand, *becoming*, the concept of which we have examined on the preceding pages, arises from the opposition of forces, and is just another word for the general struggle of forces against one another. Both conceptions agree that there are no fixed things, no permanent states; but the system allows laws of probability, which allow the outcome of the struggle to be foreseen in the individual cases. The laws of Nature are "formulas for relations of power." Something similar would be inconceivable in the Dionysian world. This world is in no way accessible to cognition, and if it is to be characterized, only aesthetic terms prove to be adequate: it is a world that always finds its way back from dissonance to harmony — returning from abundance to the simple, from the play of contradictions back to the pleasure of harmony." Such a world can never be represented philosophically, and it is impossible to fight the world in this Dionysian world of "eternal self-creation, eternal self-destruction, this mysterious world of double lust," to recognize again, as we found it described above, that world of opposition and tension, which is ruled by the strict law of unity, of justice, which *results from this tension.* "Dynamic quanta, in tension with all other dynamic quanta"[93]—that is Nietzsche's formula for the world. On the basis of this formula he has built up a physics and physiology, a psychology and an ethics. He could never have done this with the help of his Dionysism.

The question arises as to whether the entire understanding of Nietzsche up to this point, enticed by the whistle of the Dionysian pied piper, has not gone the wrong way. Time and again one has sought and found the Dionysian in Nietzsche, and *overlooked* the *philosopher*, the real friend of the Greeks, the *pupil of Heraclitus.* But when Nietzsche

---

93   *The Will to Power*, §635.

himself thinks about the ways in which he tried to prove the innocence of becoming, he does not mention Dionysus at all. To himself
he is the thinker of the Heraclitic world, *not* the disciple of Dionysus.
The name *Dionysus* is only a sign of the countermovement the young
Nietzsche initiated against Christian morality; Dionysus is identified
as a mask of the "Antichrist" in the later preface to *The Birth of Tragedy*.
For how else could he effectively name that "counter-valuation": "As
a philologist and a man of words, I christened her, not without some
freedom — for who knew the right name of the *Antichrist*? — with the
name of a Greek god: I called her the *Dionysian*."

Religious inventors and mythologists tend to be enthusiasts.
Nietzsche understood the philosopher as the *opposite* of the enthusiast. "There is nothing of a founder of religion in me."[94] But just
as the unforeseen loneliness of this singular life brought with it the
Heraclitic student's transformation into the poet Zarathustra, so the
fight against Christian Europe also brought with it the philosopher's
need to reach for symbols to say more loudly what no one wanted to
hear. How grateful he was for every sign that made it possible for him
to communicate — so he invented "Dionysus against the crucified."
*Ecce Homo* ends with this opposition. The story does not end here,
however; Nietzsche's statement on Christian Europe and its salvation
resides in *The Will to Power*.

## Note

With this presentation I complete the review of Nietzsche's concept
of the Dionysian that I began in the introduction to the Bachofen
edition by my friend Manfred Schröter. One has otherwise tried to
approach Nietzsche's thought through the concept of *myth*. However,
I have shown that *The Birth of Tragedy* does not reveal any deeper

---

94  *Ecce Homo*, "Why I Am A Fate."

relationship to the religious-mythical sphere, but rather that it clearly shows its origin in the spirit of modern music.[95]

After Nietzsche's relationship to myth was clarified, Nietzsche's other Greek writings could be duely appreciated; I identified the concept of the *agonal*, which is the opposite of the *mythical*, as the root of Nietzsche's Greco-German groundwork.[96] The present work contains the completion of what I indicated in *Bachofen and Nietzsche*.

In the introduction to the thin-print edition of his works (published by Kröner Verlag), I tried to build Nietzsche's life and figure out of two opposing basic instincts: a philosophical and a musical one. It was particularly important to me to make transparent the exceptional position of *Zarathustra* in Nietzsche's life and the peculiar form of this special work. You will find the dualism of "philosophy" and "music" I have identified in the opposition of the Heraclitic and Dionysian worlds. Because the doctrine of the Eternal Return *is music* — we would know, even if Nietzsche did not tell us himself with the words: "But know this! — that transitoriness sings its short song over and over again, and that hearing of the first verse almost dies of yearning at the thought that it would be over forever." So Dionysus has two faces: from the *music* point of view, from Wagner's point of view, he appears Greek, he appears as *Dionysos philosophos*; seen from Heraclitus, it turns out to be a musical phenomenon. Because of this ambiguity of the "Dionysian," it is not possible to understand Nietzsche beyond this concept. In this way, one only gets into the confusing problematic of Nietzschean existence.

---

95 *The Myth of the Orient and Occident* (1926), §241 ff. My demarcation between the worlds of Bachofen and Nietzsche caused Thomas Mann to try to defend Nietzsche in the "Paris Account" and elsewhere. It is not worth going into his polemics: it is one of his futile efforts.

96 *Bachofen and Nietzsche* (1929).

# II. The Politician

## 1. Germanic Attitude. Relationship with Rome

THE KEY TO UNDERSTANDING all of Nietzsche's concrete demands and goals lies in his view of the state. He didn't systematically develop it, but we can reliably reconstruct it. Here, too, there is no sign of contradiction and fluctuation: his view was consistent from beginning to end.

Nietzsche's basic concept of the state is *Germanic* and not *German*, if by *German* we want to understand the ultimate form of what has grown on Germanic soil under Christian-Roman influence in the course of our history. The constant tension in which Nietzsche finds himself with regard to "Germany" is based on the fact that he goes back to the Germanic subsoil of the German character with an imperturbability and strength like no one before him.

The area of *German* does not coincide with that of the *Germanic*. There are other peoples who participate in the *Germanic*. But wherever *German* reaches an historical climax, the *Germanic* element comes through with particular strength. Such highlights include the time of the Saxon, Frankish, and Swabian emperors; the Lutheran Reformation; and the meeting of Bismarck and Nietzsche in the 19th century. The fate of Germany can be recognized by the following facts: we were the leading political power in Europe until the death of Henry VI[1] in the most powerful period of the Middle Ages — but no permanent state was founded. We are making the great revolution that will *end* the Middle Ages — but we are leaving the benefit of it to the papacy and the Roman peoples. A statesman ultimately unites a large part of the German tribes — but the state he founded lacks inner truth: when Luther and Henry VI are juxtaposed, there is no German state that binds them. The old Germanic defiance that resists the state is overcome by Bismarck; but at the same time this defiance lives on in Nietzsche, as strong as it did a thousand years earlier, and comes into opposition with the new state.

Nietzsche called himself the "last anti-political German" in *Ecce Homo*. He felt himself to be the last German to vigorously protest against the state. His aversion to young people belongs to the state, not just to the German state, but to the state itself. The "On the Future of Our Educational Institutions" series of speeches, which he gave in Basel in the winter of 1871–1872, are directed against the "uniform state culture." And in one of his last works he says: culture and the state are antagonists — the "cultural state" is just a modern idea. "One lives off the other, one thrives at the expense of the other. All great times of culture are times of political decline: what is great in the sense of culture was apolitical, even anti-political..."[2] It makes sense to look for an aesthetic motive behind this emphasis on "culture," to assume that it is the artist in him who has revolted against state-regulated education and against all state centralization in general. In truth, the reasons for this opposition are deeper: Germanic need for freedom, Germanic-warrior pride and defiance are alive in Nietzsche when he defends himself against the state, which he perceives as an un-German, Roman institution.

---

1    Heinrich VI (d. 1197) was King of Germany and Holy Roman Emperor. His father was Frederick Barbarossa and was thus a member of the Hohenstaufen dynasty. [trans.]

2    *Twilight of the Idols*, "What the Germans Lack," §4.

In "Prowlings [*Streifzüge*] of an Untimely Man," this most important section of the *Twilight of the Idols*, Nietzsche developed his concept of freedom in a few hasty sentences. *Freedom*, he says, is not an institution: there are no liberal institutions, no liberal state. "The liberal institutions immediately cease to be liberal as soon as they are established: there is no worse and more thorough damage done to freedom than through liberal institutions." Such institutions lead to leveling — they make you small, cowardly, and indulgent. As long as they still have to be fought for, the same institutions produce completely different effects: it is war that produces these effects. *War educates people to freedom.* Because war educates people to take responsibility, *it rends great distances between those who prove themselves and those who do not* — it gets one used to toil, hardship, and privation; it makes people indifferent to life and leads to a readiness to sacrifice. *Freedom* means, in a word, "that manly instincts, which are happy and victorious, have dominion over other instincts, for example over those of 'happiness' … A free man is a warrior." Freedom is measured in individuals, as in peoples, according to a resistance that has to be overcome, according to the effort it takes to stay on top. *Individuals and peoples never grow up under liberal institutions*: great danger makes something of them. "One must need to be strong, otherwise one will never become strong." In "aristocratic communities" like Rome (as a city) or Venice, man becomes strong; the state, on the other hand, is just a breeding ground for herd animals.

It is clear enough: Nietzsche affirms war, but denies the state. This is most sharply expressed in *Zarathustra*, where the speech "On War and Warriors" is followed by the speech "On the New Idol," by which the state is to be understood. "One can only be silent and sit still when one has a bow and arrow: otherwise one gossips and quarrels… War and courage have done more great things than charity" — thus spoke Zarathustra. But then he says: "The state is called the coldest of all cold monsters." The state means the death of peoples; everything is wrong with it, it is the idol of perdition. Zarathustra does not always speak well of "the people," but here, in the face of the state, he praises them: "Where a people yet exist, they do not understand the state and hate it as an evil eye and destroyer of morals and rights... Every people speaks its language of good and evil: no neighbor will understand it. His speech was invented in morals and rights. But the state lies in all tongues of good and evil." Isn't it strange to see Zarathustra as a defender of "the people's" rights? Why has there never been a firmly established German state? Because, in the Germanic view, the king is not an emperor, but only a military leader and protector of law. Under threat, the Teuton recognized only a *Führer*, not a *master*. In peace-time, the king had the right to protect the people, nothing more. What a genuinely Germanic sentiment is Zarathustra's defense of the people against the state, of the warrior against the official! Nietzsche is not aware that he is expressing the secret of German history; nor does he speak from historical knowledge, but from the immediacy of instinct. From the same immediacy, the young Nietzsche saw Germanic and Romanesque, Greek and Roman beings over and against each other. The state as we know it is an invention of the Orient. The Romans assumed it from the Orient and cultivated it; the *Imperium Romanum* (to be distinguished from the "aristocratic community" of republican Rome) means the completion of the entire Mediterranean culture. That comprehensive system of order we have called the "state" since then, with its imperial center, its centralized administrative apparatus, its claim to submission and obedience, *is something alien to the North*. The life of the Germanic peoples is based on clan and militaristic as-sociation; law and war are the two sides of this life; law and war are not merged into a unified, universal structure. And the same aversion to the universalism of the state we notice among the Germanic peoples we find in the Greek people, who are related to the Germanic peoples and for whom Nietzsche had the greatest admiration. The Greeks created the greatest war epic in the world; but the *Iliad* does not corre-spond to any Greek state. There are only small Greek states, city-states, which live in incessant feuds with one another. With what pleasure

Nietzsche's gaze rests on the spectacle of this incessant struggle, on this "bloody jealousy from town to town, from party to party, this murderous greed of those little wars, the tiger-like triumph over the corpse of the slain enemy — in short, the incessant renewal of those Trojan battles and atrocities." *There* was a people — that was the great experience of the young Nietzsche — who accepted the existing drive for power and victory and considered it *justified*. "The struggle and the lust for victory were recognized: and nothing separates the Greek world so much from ours as the coloring of individual ethical concepts derived from this, for example *strife* and *envy*." The Christianized world only knows envy as an evil or petty emotion; in the Greek world, envy means the urge to assert yourself — to *power*, to *victory*. It is this drive that Nietzsche presented in his main philosophical work as the basis of the entire world. In praise of the Greeks, he said at last in *Twilight of the Idols*: "I saw their strongest instinct, the *will to power*, I saw them tremble before the irrepressible violence of this drive — I saw all their institutions grow out of protective measures around themselves to guard against each other's own internal explosiveness."[3] The form of life of the Greek man, the form of exertion, of the incessant struggle to be "the best and superior to others," is based on this drive. This is exactly the meaning of the Germanic principality: because *a prince is not whoever heads a bureaucratic apparatus, but who is first in danger and in battle.*

Nietzsche recognized with decisive clarity the opposition between the Greek and Roman characters in relation to the state. In his Greek book one view falls on the Roman state: the Roman Empire is equated with the "extreme secularization," which is called its greatest, most terrifying expression (*The Birth of Tragedy*). We read of a senseless state expansion of the *Imperium Romanum* in the preparatory work on *The Will to Power*, and of an abuse of power by the Roman emperors, through which the slave-morality of the powerless came to victory.

---

3    "What I Owe The Ancients," §3. [trans.]

For Nietzsche, the system of competition, with its squandering of all strength, stands higher than the system of the state, with its frugality, which regards any agonal waste of strength as "useless." And how sharply Nietzsche expresses himself in the middle of his path when he writes in *Human, All Too Human*: "The crude Roman patriotism is now, when completely different and higher tasks than *patria* and *honos* [country and honor] are set, either something dishonest or a sign of *backwardness*."[4] How old-Germanic is this word![5] The image of the Germanic hero as the best authority of the Nordic soul, Andreas Heusler[6] teaches us, is completely lacking in the superpersonal. There is no fatherland and no homeland for these battles; even the most admired heroic struggle of the Great Migration — the last battle of the Ostrogoths with King Teja's fall[7] — was not a struggle for "freedom and fatherland," according to him. "That one asserts oneself in some extraordinary situation and with courage, self-control, despite death defying one's warrior honor, *that* is what matters." With such words, which could be spoken by Nietzsche,[8] Heusler describes the essence of the Germanic. In the *Icelandic Sagas*,[9] the same researcher finds the perfect, realistic representation of what Nietzsche meant by his *master*-morality: that is *warrior*-morality — compared to *slave*-morality, that is servant ethics. In the epilogue to the *The Wagner Case*, Nietzsche speaks of the actual Icelandic sagas as "perhaps the most important

---

4    *Human, All Too Human*, §442.

5    That is, *backwardness* (*Zurückgebliebenheit*). [trans.]

6    Heusler (d. 1940), a Swiss philologist, specialized in Germanic studies. [trans.]

7    The Ostrogoths, led by King Teja, were all but destroyed near the slopes of Vesuvius in 553 CE. [trans.]

8    Heusler's sentiment also compares favorably with Oswald Spengler (*Man and Technics*): "We are born into this time and must bravely follow the path to the destined end. There is no other way. Our duty is to hold on to the lost position, without hope, without rescue... *That* is greatness. *That* is what it means to have race. The *honorable end* is the one thing that cannot be taken from a man." [trans.]

9    Heusler wrote two books on the Icelandic sagas: one in 1911, one in 1914. [trans.]

document" of men's morality. The Old Norse language has the word *mikilmenni*, which means "man of great kind," *master*-man. Generosity in the *will to power*, as well as an inclination to give and help, indicates greatness. "Opposite him is the *litilmenni*: the *Lützelmann*, the man of small size, who is afraid of everyone and who regrets the gift." It is as if it were taken from *Genealogy of Morals*. And this sentence of Heusler's sounds like it comes from *The Antichrist*: "In order to name the new virtue of *humility* Germanic, one had to resort to root words that meant *lowly* or *servant*; *humility* was indeed, according to the older view, a *servant* disposition." And, finally, it looks like a motto for Nietzsche's fight against compassionate morality and pacifist humanitarianism when Heusler says, characteristically: "Instead of general human obligations, there was a great dichotomy into *friends* and *un-friends*."[10]

It could be objected that Nietzsche judged the Romans and Greeks quite differently in *Twilight of the Idols*. In the section "What I Owe the Ancients," he praises Sallust and Horace[11] as the writers from whom he learned to write. "You will recognize, right into my *Zarathustra*, a very serious ambition after the Roman style, in the '*aere perenium*'[12] style." He added that he did not owe any similarly strong impressions to the Greeks; they cannot be to us what the Romans are. Of course, Nietzsche praises Thucydides[13] with the same breath. The passage is completely misunderstood when it is related to the Romans *per se*: only the Romans are meant as literary models, as masters of elegant form, of

---

10   The quoted passages come from Heusler's contribution — "Old Germanic Morale and Wisdom" — in the anthology *Germanic Resurrection* (Heidelberg, 1926), edited by H. Nollau, 195, 200. [trans.]

11   Sallust was a Roman historian and politician from a plebeian family. His writing is characterized by its incisiveness. Horace was the preeminent poet under Augustus. [trans.]

12   Or *aere perennius* — "more lasting than bronze." Horace boasts, in the final poem of *Odes*, that his poetry will outlast any manmade monument: *Exegi monumentum aere perennius. — I have made a monument more lasting than bronze.* [trans.]

13   Author of *History of the Peloponnesian War*, Thucydides was a Greek (Athenian) historian and general. [trans.]

perfect literary attitude. There is no doubt Nietzsche learned the essentials from them. It is to this school that he owes the hammered polish of his style, which stands in marked contrast to the content of his philosophy. But it can never be inferred from Nietzsche's attitude towards Roman literature that he was unsure of his Germanic-Greek instincts. The content of his teaching is *un*-Roman, even *anti*-Roman — this is expressed most strongly in his hostility to the state as an institution.

Incidentally, there is ample evidence Nietzsche was aware of this close relationship with the Nordic, warlike world, as he generally demonstrates an uncanny genius in tracking down his kith or contenders. At a time when the Icelandic sagas were still unknown to broader circles, he described the "noble man," the mighty man of the saga, "who has power over himself, who knows how to speak and remain silent, who exercises severity and harshness towards himself with pleasure and has reverence before all rigor and harshness."[14] He also speaks of the German nobility as "fundamentally Viking nobility,"[15] and there is also a reference to the Vikings in the *Nachlaß*. They are likened with the people of the Renaissance. Instead of Nietzsche's "Renaissance-ism," one should rather speak of his *Germanism*, which coincides with his Greek fighting-ethic and fighting-metaphysic. Moreover, the nobility in the upper and central Italian city-states, which, in their feuding, produced the type that Nietzsche admires, most likely came from Germanic blood. That admiration was kindled not by the art of the Renaissance, but by the warlike-agonal nature of the epoch.

Aesthetes and aesthetically minded writers have propagated the opinion that Nietzsche's admiration for power and warlike nature was born solely from the experiences of a wistful dreamer, a cultivated sentimentalist who, conscious of his own impotence, was intoxicated by images of power and cruelty. A famous textbook in the history of philosophy says of this admiration with inimitable seriousness: "It is

---

14  *Beyond Good and Evil*, §260.

15  *The Antichrist*, §60. [trans.]

the nervous professor who would like to be a savage tyrant." This kind of psychological interpretation overlooks the fact that Nietzsche does *not* subjectively glorify power, but describes types, forms of life that really existed in history — breeding systems on a natural basis. Nietzsche resurrects something that was buried in the depths of our past, something whose traces can also be found elsewhere. It is something objective, something that has always been potent and has come to life again in Nietzsche that has led him to his deep insights. Aesthetic rhapsody does not have such results.

## 2. The Antichrist. Protestantism and Catholicism

If one wants to understand Nietzsche's relationship to Christianity correctly, one must never disregard the fact that the decisive sentence "God is dead" is an *historical* statement. Nietzsche does not fight the Christian churches and Christian doctrine with the fatal subjectivism of the know-it-all zealots, but with realistic arguments: he shows what it really looks like in "Christian" Europe. The criticism of slave-morality and the destruction of priestly values are inseparable from a realistic view of history. The historical view of things is part of every true realism; Heracliticism is perfected in the perception of events as fateful. Theology is being replaced by the philosophy of history. The question of the *history* of Christianity is inseparable from the question of Christianity. Here, too, in the last and deepest layer, we encounter Nietzsche's Germanism. *The doctrine of the downfall of the gods comes from the North.* "I believe in the ancient Germanic saying: all gods must die," we read in the drafts for *The Birth of Tragedy*. If one holds the sentence "God is dead" next to this saying of the young Nietzsche, one sees Zarathustra's task. This is his mission: *to proclaim the death of the Christian God out of the Germanic substance.* Zarathustra means the fulfillment of the premonition that lies in the saying: all gods must die.

From here alone the tremendous seriousness that lies in Nietzsche's work and phenomenon becomes visible and understandable.

In *The Birth of Tragedy*, the young Nietzsche contrasts the "alien myth" of Christianity with the "native myth," which alone is capable of educating. Half a generation later, during a long review of his work, he says of the same youthful writing: "In this book, the transplantation of a deeply *anti-German myth*, the *Christian*, into the German heart is considered the real German undoing." This sentence is not only decisive for understanding the politician Nietzsche — it also reveals the secret of Nietzsche's relationship with Wagner, which is so important for mankind. "I just want to admit it," says a note from the time of *Human, All Too Human*,[16] "I had hoped that art would have completely spoiled the Germans for stale Christianity — German mythology as weakening, getting used to polytheism, etc. What a horror over restorative currents!" That Wagner became Christian with *Parsifal* was the decisive factor and led to a final break. In *Parsifal*, Nietzsche sensed the spirit of the Counter-Reformation. It seemed to him the abyss of mendacity that the same man who had conceived the figure of Siegfried finally sank before the cross and the priest. In a detailed note of his *Nachlaß*, Nietzsche relates the "hysterical-erotic trait" Wagner particularly loved in women and set to music of French Romanticism, and he predicts the Parisians will inevitably convert to Wagner one day — one of Nietzsche's numerous correct predictions. He feels that the hysterical-erotic trait is thoroughly un-German and therefore doubts Wagner was a German artist. But *something* about Wagner is German, he suspects — maybe his strength and boldness, or that he lived with such stark discipline, on his own as a relentless atheist, antinomist and immoralist, or that he invented the figure of a very free person, Siegfried, "which may indeed be too free, too hard, too good-natured, too un-Christian for the Latin taste?" The Latin taste, the Roman world, has a deep affinity for Christianity — that is

---

16   Circa 1878, or around ten years before Nietzsche's collapse. [trans.]

a fundamental belief for Nietzsche. In the Roman-dominated modern culture, he sees the "feeling of Protestantism" extinguished; he realizes a real preponderance of Catholicism. Even so, decidedly "anti-Protestant movements" like Wagner's *Parsifal* are no longer perceived as such within this culture. And with an abrupt turn in profundity, Nietzsche continues this train of thought: "The whole higher spirituality in France is Catholic in instinct; Bismarck has understood that Protestantism no longer exists."[17]

This is the principal aspect under which Nietzsche sees Protestantism: it is a movement against Romanism, as something that comes from the North. Before exploring this, however, we will finish discussing the Roman world. An aphorism of *The Dawn* is decisive for this; here Nietzsche speaks of the French under the title "Desire for Perfect Opponents."[18] The aphorism is written out of that wonderful chivalrous mood in which the fighter honors his opponent because he knows that he is doing *himself* the greatest honor. "One cannot deny that the French were the most Christian people on earth..." is how this wonderful description begins; and it ends with the statement that this people of "perfect Christian types" also had to produce the perfect counter-types of the un-Christian free spirit.

Here a little foray into the field of Nietzsche-interpretation becomes necessary. Nietzsche wrote several of his books under the sign of the "free spirit": *Human, All Too Human, The Dawn, The Joyful Wisdom, Beyond Good and Evil*. The way in which he contrasts this type with German clumsiness and dishonesty has led some to see a turn to a an acceptance of French forms of expression — a turning away from German spirituality, indeed a conversion to Romanism in general. The *type* of free spirit is un-German — "free spirit" is just a translation of the expression *libre penseur* [free thinker]. This type has a different culture than the German one — it is the *antithesis* to the most perfect types of Latin Christianity, as Nietzsche teaches us.

Great pains have been taken to prove Nietzsche's Romanism. His veneration of the French moralists' aphoristic books, especially thos of La Rochefoucauld,[19] plays a major role in this. However, let us remember the fact that this veneration is by no means without substantial reservations. The Christian origin La Rochefoucauld's moralism — and the establishment of this origin *always* means an objection with Nietzsche — was clear to Nietzsche very early on: La Rochefoucauld, like Pascal, is an *opponent*. Both have "the whole Greek taste against them," and La Rochefoucauld exposes the ugliness of man "per the instructions of Christianity." For Nietzsche, a conversion to Romanism, even in its free-spirited, moralistic form, should have always meant a decline to Christianity — the proponents of his "Romanism" did not make this consequence clear to themselves. They did not recognize that Nietzsche's inclination towards Romanism is essentially an *antithesis* — an effective mask to irritate, ridicule, and frighten the satisfied Germans of the "Reich."[20]

The moment one tries to explain Nietzsche's hostility to Christianity with the help of the term "free spirit," one loses sight of the real reasons for his anti-Christianism. From Bernhard to Fénelon and Chateaubriand, French Christianity is *sentimental* — taking this word in its most objective sense. The counterattack against Roman, effeminate Christianity is therefore always based on reason: the free spirit fights emotional religion from the position of reason. So if one really wanted to see Nietzsche as a free spirit, one would have to call Nietzsche a *rationalist* at the same time. *He is not.* We ignore his irrationalist metaphysics entirely: the attack on Christianity which he is leading is also decisively misunderstood if one sees in it only an attack in the manner of Voltaire. Nietzsche sometimes thought of the

---

19  François de La Rochefoucauld (d. 1680) was a French writer and moralist. [trans.]

20  That is, the Second Reich under Bismarck. [trans.]

anti-Christianity of this man whom he had deliberately portrayed as his champion in the era of *Human, All Too Human* with a certain pity. He felt, with cutting clarity, his own position was infinitely more daring, infinitely more dangerous than that of the boldest rationalist opponent of the church in the 18th century. Nietzsche approaches Christianity not with cool, mocking superiority, not out of luxury and skepticism. He comes to it with fate in his heart: *all gods must die.* This is not the belief of a free spirit! A free spirit does not say: "God is dead," he says: "If God did not exist, one would have to invent him."[21] Everything free-spirited, everything ridiculous and skeptical is only *a means to an end* for Nietzsche. Behind the mask of the free spirit stands the tremendous seriousness of those who see a fate hovering over the world in which they live and who know they are destined to be the first to name this fate.

We complete this proof of Nietzsche's anti-Romanism by saying: it is not Latin free-spiritedness, but *Siegfried* driving Nietzsche's attack on Christianity. Nordic paganism is the immeasurable, dark underground from which the bold fighter against Christian Europe emerges. He sees Christianity as rooted in the Latin races. "It seems that the Latin races are far more attached to their Catholicism than we Northerners are attached to Christianity generally..."[22] In Catholic countries, then, disbelief means "a kind of revolt against the spirit of the race, while with us it is rather a return to the spirit (or non-spirit) of the race."[23] This return or "non-spirit" is to be taken very seriously, because Nietzsche means that "we Northerners," compared to the inhabitants of Romanized regions, are really barbarians. With what force does his barbarian blood stir in the face of Renan's mawkish language, how does he immediately discover our "probably less beautiful and harder, namely, *more German* soul." The *sickness* of the will which has

---

21  Voltaire, *Épître à l'Auteur du Livre des Trois Imposteurs* (1769/70). [trans.]

22  *Beyond Good and Evil*, §48.

23  *Beyond Good and Evil*, §48. [trans.]

come to Europe as a result of Christianity shows itself greatest and most varied where civilization has long been established[24]; the will is thus most seriously ill in what is now France, for here we are the furthest removed from northern barbarism.

Of all the problems in understanding Nietzsche, it is certain his concept of *Germanness* contains the greatest difficulties. At no point in his work is one confronted with such an abundance of contradictions. So would those who want to deny Nietzsche a unified view be right after all? No! With careful and patient examination, the ostensible contradictions can all be derived from a uniform conception. One only has to consider Nietzsche's personal situation, especially the situation after the publication of *Zarathustra*, and, secondly, one must remember that all the main lines of his thought are intertwined in the problem of the "German nature." For Germany has been exposed to ruin for millennia, and Nietzsche, as a Nordic man, sees disaster in this. Germany is also a part of *Christian* Europe — against which he *fought*. Above all, the interweaving of the "German" with the "Christian" must be noted. Nietzsche makes all important statements about the Germans from this point of view: What role do the Germans play in the Christianization of Europe?

Apart from a few, albeit telling and important passages, Nietzsche speaks of the Germans with utter displeasure. But do not misinterpret this displeasure! It is a disappointment about the lack of German spirituality or morality; it is not a displeasure over German *nature*, but German *history* — it is an historical displeasure. It is based on the observation that the Germans were obliged to become the first un-Christian people in Europe. They are still deeply rooted in "Nordic barbarism"; they are actually *the* warlike people of Europe; they have produced the greatest enemy of the Church; they are the people in whom a figure like Siegfried in *Der Ring des Nibelungen* could be conceived: so how is it possible that they are *still* Christians? All of

---

24 *Beyond Good and Evil*, §208.

Nietzsche's statements about Germany should be read from this point of view.

"German Hopes" is the title of the central aphorism of *The Joyful Wisdom*, which we must cite here in full.

> Let us not forget that the names of peoples are usually names of contempt. The *Tatars*, for example, are, after their name, 'the dogs': this is how the Chinese christened them. The *Deutschen* [Germans]: this originally means *heathen*; this is what the converted Goths called their unbaptized tribesmen, according to their translation of the Septuagint, in which the heathen are referred to with the word, which in Greek means 'the peoples' — see Ulfilas. It would still be possible for the Germans to make an honorable name of their old epithet by becoming the first *un-Christian* people in Europe: for which purpose Schopenhauer, to their honor, regarded them as highly qualified. Thus the work of Luther, who taught them to be non-Roman, would be realized, and they would say: *Here I stand! I cannot do otherwise!*

These pertinent lines, in particular, are un-Roman: *Here I stand! I cannot do otherwise!* The way in which the individual stands defiant, with his fate, does not fit with Latin universalism, with the state-consciousness of the Roman man, who knows he is always bound to an institution, arranged in a reasonably governed whole, held by forms and traditions. Zarathustra's anti-Roman, anti-state tendency is linked to his hostility to the church, this "last Roman building." "'Church? What is that?' — 'Church?' I replied, 'It is a kind of state, and the most mendacious.'"[25] It is not a passing idea when Nietzsche relates church and state to one another; rather, this link goes back to the deepest basis of his Germanic awareness of freedom and fate. The state's premise, as is its position, is: "the limit is reached." The state's principle is that of *shaping*, which *hinders* the freedom and growth of the individual. The state based on the Roman model and the church, which has realized this model most perfectly, is in his eyes a means of uniforming people, of *alienating them from their fate*. This interpretation comes from a

---

25   *Zarathustra*, "On Great Events."

passage in the preliminary work on *The Will to Power*, which reads: "Prerequisite for prior states: man should not develop — the limit is reached! The Catholic Church (the oldest of all forms of government in Europe) now best represents the old state!"

If this is recognized and accepted, then it is clear: no figure in German history can be more attractive and provocative for Nietzsche than Luther.

E. Hirsch has shown that Nietzsche's image of Luther is dependent on Janssen's[26] interpretation in his "History of the German People"; Ch. Andler[27] has shown how Ranke[28] influenced Nietzsche's conception of Protestantism. One cannot expect a picture of Luther drawn from the sources — in this respect every student of theology is superior to the author of *The Antichrist*. Nietzsche does not speak of Luther from historical knowledge, but rather speaks of him from a related historical situation: as a man who, in the reality of events, stands at a corresponding point within *German*, even *European*, events.

Luther is celebrated as the "great benefactor" in *The Dawn*[29] because he has shaken the monk's way of life, the Christian *vita contemplativa* [contemplative life], and thus made the path to an un-Christian *vita contemplativa* accessible again. But Nietzsche does not completely yield to Luther: the reformer has only replaced the building of the Catholic Church, this noble Roman building, with another, coarser and more

---

26  Johannes Janssen (d. 1891) was a German (Roman Catholic) historian; he argued that Martin Luther's Reformation had deleterious effects on Germany. [trans.]

27  Charles Andler (d. 1933) was a French (Protestant) philosopher who was denied his philosophy professorship for showing bias toward German thought; he eventually became a professor of German. In addition to his work on Nietzsche, he wrote *Pan Germanism: Its Plans for German Expansion in the World* (1915). [trans.]

28  Leopold von Ranke (d. 1886) was a German (Protestant) historian who coined the term *Counter-Reformation*. He ran an anti-liberalism journal, *Historische-Politische Zeitschrift*, and often argued against the ideas and outcomes of the French Revolution. [trans.]

29  §88.

modest church building. That old building rests on a foundation that can also be characterized thusly: "it rests on a *Southern* freedom and liberalism of spirit, and also on a *Southern* suspicion of Nature, man, and spirit — it rests on a completely different knowledge and experience of man than the *North* has had. In all its breadth, the Lutheran Reformation was simplicity's indignation towards something "diverse." To speak cautiously, it was a coarse, honest misunderstanding for which much is to be forgiven — one misunderstood the expression of a victorious Church and saw only corruption; one misunderstood the noble skepticism, that *luxury* of skepticism and tolerance which every victorious, self-assured power allows itself..."[30] The aphorism from which these sentences are taken is entitled: "The Peasant Revolt of the Spirit." This means the Reformation is held responsible for the degeneration of the modern scholar and for German honesty in matters of knowledge — in short, for the *plebeianism* of the last centuries.

The more fiercely Nietzsche rages against the Germans, the more sharply he speaks about Luther and the Reformation. The germane aphorism is in the fifth book of *The Joyful Wisdom*, which was developed simultaneously with *Beyond Good and Evil* and is already completely overshadowed by the mood from which the writings of the last creative year emerged. *The Wagner Case*, *Twilight of the Idols*, *The Antichrist*, and *Ecce Homo* are essentially nothing more than attacks on Germany. This attack also includes taking sides *with* the Catholic Church, against which the new Germany (in the *Kulturkampf*) has just lost a battle.[31] It is also not difficult to see why Nietzsche defends the church: it is a magnificent power structure, and thus admirable. For the same reason, the *Imperium Romanum* is occasionally recognized in the last writings. Admiration for "noble skepticism" is one of Nietzsche's weapons against the German spirit, which is incapable of skepticism. How ambiguous the text immediately becomes when Nietzsche begins

---

30  *The Joyful Wisdom*, §358.

31  This could refer to any number of so-called Mitigation Laws passed between 1878–1887 granting more concessions to the Church. [trans.]

to praise the church is evident from that little peasant-revolt aphorism: "It seems that the Germans do not understand the essence of a church." In fact, given Nietzsche's own presuppositions, you cannot understand it. The sentence can only express a rebuke in this context — but in this sense, it is surely *praise*.[32]

Nietzsche's most trenchant polemics can be found in *The Antichrist* and *Ecce Homo* — and in both cases, they counter Christianity in the North and the Germans. The mere fact that there is a *Christianity of the North*, a Protestantism, is enough for Nietzsche. If there has to be Christianity, then it belongs to the peoples among whom it originated and first spread. *It is a product of the Mediterranean world and therefore foreign to the Germanic North from the start.* "If one wants to assert that the Teuton was formed and predetermined for Christianity, one must not lack insolence. For the opposite is not only true, but also palpable. How should the invention of those two excellent Jews, Jesus and Saul — *the two most Jewish Jews that possibly ever existed* — have been more at home with the Germanic peoples than with other peoples?" This is how Nietzsche wrote at the time of *The Dawn*. Europe has allowed an "excess of oriental morality," he says, to proliferate within itself. And in the eye of the young Nietzsche, who is used to the clarity of the Greek world, the history of the West is reflected as follows: "The weakened Greek culture, Romanized, coarsened, become *decorative*, then accepted as a *decorative* culture by a weakened Christianity as an ally, and spread with violence among uncivilized peoples — that is the history of Western culture. The trick has been achieved — the Greek and the sanctimonious have been united." That this view of the contrast between Mediterranean culture and its religions and the spirit of the Germanic North was alive in Nietzsche to the very end is testified by his most important late work, *Genealogy of Morals*. The basic idea: Mediterranean culture has its climax in the *priestly* type, who corresponds to a way of life in which *pathos* and *resentment* are

---

32  *The Joyful Wisdom*, §358. [trans.]

combined — priests are the best *haters* and know how to solemnly express their hatred. The warlike form of the Teutons, which is related to the Greek, is of the opposite nature — the Greeks play such a unique role in the history of the Mediterranean peoples because, unlike the Romans, *they never succumbed to the influence of the Orient.* A fleeting note by Nietzsche clearly shows us both worlds: "The heroic man who rests from the struggle, the hardships, and hatred and is ashamed of pathos — and then there's the priest!"

Nietzsche's last writings — *Genealogy* and *The Antichrist* — are devoted to the psychology of the priest. Nietzsche's work is consummated in the attack on this counter-warrior type, in the analysis of man who dares to bless and curse in the name of the *Most High God.* In the priest he sees the inventor and guardian of guilt, the man who rules by dominating the guilty conscience of others. In an attack of unprecedented force, Nietzsche proves the heroic way of life he professes a philosopher. One does not say that he should have represented the ideal of the hero *psychologically*; if the heroic man mattered, he could not represent him psychologically, for all psychology disparages. For Nietzsche, psychology is always just a weapon. The fact that he only occasionally and briefly describes the warrior type prevents lesser readers from seeing. But those who do not understand *Genealogy of Morals* miss the key to Nietzsche's final findings.

Nietzsche's narrowing interests in this late period culminate in two sentences of *The Antichrist*: "I don't understand how a German could ever feel Christian ..."[33] and "If mankind never manages to get rid of Christianity, the Germans will be to blame ..."[34] After the preceding, these exclamations explain themselves — you can hear the cracking voice in the last one. Everything that Nietzsche said against Luther, against the Reformation, against the Germans — it always goes back to only one reproach: *they prevented the fall of Christianity.* "Cesare Borgia

---

33   *The Antichrist*, §60. [trans.]

34   *The Antichrist*, §61. [trans.]

as Pope"[35] would have been the end — the anger of Luther's peasants did not allow that: the Reformation only brought about a new rise of the papacy, made the triumph of the Counter-Reformation possible. "It was the Germans who caused Europe to lose the fruits, the whole meaning of her last great period — *the Renaissance.* At a moment when a higher order of values, noble values, values that said *yes* to life, and that guaranteed a future, had succeeded in triumphing over the opposite values, the values of degeneration, in the very seat of Christianity itself — and even in the hearts of those sitting there — Luther, that disaster of a monk, restored the Church and, what is a thousand times worse, Christianity, at the very moment it was defeated... Catholics have cause to celebrate *Luther festivals*, to compose *Luther plays...*"[36]

Almost everything Nietzsche says about the Reformation is negative. It is precisely from this fact that we recognize Nietzsche's historical position. Because he does not want to revert pre-Reformation circumstances, but rather wants to move beyond them, this will *must* be expressed negatively. From his point of view, the Reformation only hindered development. He constructs a possible dialectical course in which the papacy would have canceled itself through its secularity — but this, of course, is a highly dubious assumption. It is at least clear Nietzsche takes a decided stance against the Reformation. This is the source of those notorious judgments, which read as condemnations of the German spirit. But if one understands the context, it is demonstrably clear that Nietzsche is only dealing in *antitheses*, and not

---

35   Cesare Borgia (d. 1507) was an Italian cardinal and military leader (having renounced the former to pursue the latter). He is thought to be an inspiration for Machiavelli's *The Prince.* Mentioning Borgia in §46 and §61, Nietzsche seems to suggest that Borgia, a contemporary of Martin Luther, would have brought revolutionary changes to Christendom had he survived his military exploits and won the papacy. Luther, however, "raised a rebellion against the Renaissance in Rome." The Renaissance, for Nietzsche, was the transvaluation of Christian values. [trans.]

36   *Ecce Homo,* "Why I Write Such Excellent Books," §2; compare to *The Antichrist,* §61. [trans.]

taking sides with the Mediterranean priesthood and the old church, which is *impossible* for him. The assessment of the *Imperium Romanum* in his last writings offers a parallel to this. As soon as Nietzsche rushes against the priestly system with full force, even the political system of the Romans shines in transfigured splendor. In *Genealogy*, the aristocratic Romans are set against the Jews: "The Romans were the strong and noble ones; there has never been a stronger, nobler nation on earth; every remnant of them, every inscription enraptures, granting one can guess *what* is doing the writing."[37] In relation to Jews and Christians, Greeks and Romans move on the same level.[38] Even old rivals must get along — the *Imperium Romanum* itself receives the highest praise: "Christianity sucked the blood of the *Imperium Romanum* ... Is it still not understood? The *Imperium Romanum* ... this most admirable work of grand style, was a beginning, its construction was calculated to reveal itself over millennia; even to this day, nothing has been similarly built, nor even dreamed of building *sub specie aeterni* to the same extent!"[39]

## 3. Rousseau. Against Democracy and Socialism

One of the most profound and momentous thoughts of Nietzsche in the study of history that will one day become apparent: the modern democratic ideals, insofar as they aim at the happiness of most of the people, at the welfare state, are of Christian, Roman-Christian origin. Nietzsche did not investigate the origins of English liberalism; Calvinism is outside of his field of vision; but he followed with the greatest interest the process of transforming Roman-mystical religiosity into a political theory, which finds its conclusion in Rousseau's teachings. The Genevan, revolutionary politician, optimistic pedagogue,

---

37 *Genealogy of Morals*, Essay I, §16.

38 *The Antichrist*, §59.

39 *The Antichrist*, §58; also *Twilight of the Idols*, "Prowlings of an Untimely Man," §39.

sentimental novelist, enthusiast and rhetorician, the famous author of *The Social Contract* and *Emile*, Rousseau is Nietzsche's most intimate enemy. This enmity must be distinguished from that between Nietzsche and Plato or Nietzsche and Pascal. Such men are his equals as competitors; Rousseau, on the other hand, belongs to another type: *he is spiritually a priest*. He knows all the sleights of hand to maneuver himself into the right without fighting; he knows how to mentally kill an opponent. This does not require sacred formulas — moral terms are sufficient. The moral defamation of the opponent is Rousseau's most effective invention; he is the master of moralizing resentment: the private person as a priest, blessing and cursing, praising and condemning in the name of reason, goodness, virtue, humanity — this seductive model continues to have an effect to this day.

Nietzsche attacked Rousseau again and again, circling him like a fencer. One of the most complete psychological descriptions that his work contains could be put together solely with reference to Rousseau. He hates the Genevan because of his false, soft, Christian concept of "Nature," because of his mendacious morality. "I still hate Rousseau during the Revolution: it is the world-historical expression for this duality of idealist and *canaille*."[40] Voltaire with his pessimism, with his skepticism, and his measure is infinitely closer to him than the suspicious optimist, about whom this cutting sentence can be found in Nietzsche's *Nachlaß*: "There are people who cannot help but force a *yes* or *no* with regard to their whole being: their suffering from megalomania stems from their distrust of themselves." To characterize the priestly nature of Rousseau's doctrine, only one sentence from the masterful presentation in *The Will to Power*[41] is cited: Rousseau defends the goodness and foresight of God against Voltaire's pessimism.

---

40  That is, *scoundrel. Twilight of the Idols*, "Prowlings of an Untimely Man," §48. [trans.]

41  §95 ff.

Nietzsche remarks: "He needed God in order to be able to cast a curse on society and civilization."[42]

What Nietzsche fights above all in Rousseau is his *pity*, his *feminism*. "Rousseau, in his preference for the poor, women, and the people-as-sovereign, is entirely in the Christian movement: all slavish faults and virtues exist in him, even the most incredible mendacity (he wants to teach justice!). His counterpart: Napoleon — ancient, people-despiser." Nietzsche would perceive the modern concept of the citizen, which equates women with men politically, as a consequence of Rousseau's presuppositions.

The demand for political equality in modern democratic states *necessarily emerges from the Christian doctrine that all people are equal before God*. For Nietzsche, this doctrine contains a disorganizing principle: *it not only abolishes natural differences, but also destroys all traditions*. The democratic ideal is based on the recognition of human equality, on the belief in the eventual triumph of truth, love, and justice. Such a belief, however, is *life-destroying*, it prevents a "hierarchy of forces" from being established in which commanders command and obeyers obey. It leads to the fact that those "down on their luck," the *inferior*, the *actors* seize the great words — *freedom*, *equality*, *justice* — and set up a kind of Jesuit rule. A social condition arises in which the "merchants and middle men" play a role; the literati and the "representatives" become dominant. A press develops which has the task of diverting the ears and senses in the wrong direction, while all major political events "sneak secretly and veiled into the theater." Vaunted parliamentarism is only a means *in the service of the parties*; Nietzsche defines it as "public permission to choose between five basic political opinions."[43] Woman masculinizes herself and thus loses the position she occupies in greater, healthier times.

---

42  *The Will to Power*, §100.

43  *The Joyful Wisdom*, §174.

With a truly world-historical view, Nietzsche sees socialism[44] as a brother to despotism, because, like despotism, socialism desires an abundance of state power; indeed, it surpasses all in its striving for the formal annihilation of the individual. Man in his own way appears to him as an unjustified luxury of Nature; it is to be "reworked" into a regular organ of the community. Nietzsche clearly sees the peculiar situation in which socialism finds itself in relation to the state: socialism wants the state, it wants "the most submissive prostration of all citizens before the unconditional state" — but at the same time, it works on the elimination of all existing states. That means, we add, socialism is *hostile* to the state insofar as the state signifies an *historical* entity; but it is for every state-omnipotence insofar as the state adapts itself to its purposes. In order to achieve its goal, continues Nietzsche, socialism "drives the semi-educated masses with the word 'justice' like a nail in the head in order to completely rob them of their minds ... and for the evil game they are supposed to play to create a good conscience."[45] The conclusion is this:

> Socialism can serve to teach the danger of all accumulations of state power quite brutally and emphatically, and, to this extent, instill suspicion of the state itself. When his hoarse voice joins the field shouting: 'As much state as possible,' it initially becomes noisier than ever: but soon the opposite also comes out with all-the-greater force: 'As little state as possible.'

From these sentences, which are of programmatic importance for Nietzsche's political views, we must infer that for him the state means a crowd of private people with petty, selfish interests held together by violent measures. The concept of a state is determined by its manifestations: merchant-state, police-state, education-state. It is *not* the *great historical type of state* that Nietzsche turns against — in this area he has remarkably little experience and knowledge — it is the state-regulated society with its need for trade and earnings, enjoyment and education,

---

44  That is, *international* socialism or *materialistic* socialism (Marxism). [trans.]

45  *Human, All Too Human*, I, §473.

security and peace that he has in mind when he condemns the "modern state." "To make society theft- and fire-proof and infinitely convenient for every trade and change, and to transform the state into Providence (in the good and bad sense) — these are *low, mediocre,* and *dispensable* goals, which one should not strive for with the ablest means — means one should save for only the noblest ends..."[46]

*Human, All Too Human* is very instructive about the politician Nietzsche. Here you can already find the basic formula for the modern state that remains in effect until the end: "Modern democracy is the historical form of the decline of the state."[47] This sentence is derived at the end of a long historical meditation, whereby the relationship between "religion and government" serves as the starting point. The state, it is said, surrounds itself with the glamor of religion for its own benefit, because with the help of the priests a government "legitimizes" its power. In the concept of "above," divine and human authority merge; custodial government and preservation of religion go hand in hand. But what happens when the people become sovereign and religion is a private matter? Then society *dissolves*, the concept of the state is abolished, the opposition between private and public disappears. "The disregard, decay, and death of the state, the unleashing of the private person (I am careful not to say the *individual*), is the consequence of the democratic concept of the state; here lies its mission." The subtlety lies in the fact that Nietzsche *approves* of this development, the mission of the democratic concept of the state. If democracy fulfills its mission, then "a new page" will be turned in the storybook of mankind, and the author carefully suggests that the time *he hopes for* will then begin: the prospect that will result from this certain decay "is not an unfortunate one."

The old state goes with religion and priests; the new state, *insofar as it has democratic ideals*, is of Christian origin and is *necessarily heading*

---

46   *The Dawn,* §179.

47   §472.

*towards anarchy* — for Nietzsche, these are two acts of the same drama. One may perhaps further interpret his historical-philosophical construction as follows: where there is still the state, there is still the Middle Ages. The democratic state is the successor to the religiously supported authoritarian state. Only when this form of government passes will we be out of the Middle Ages — only then is Christianity no longer a decisive power.

Nietzsche's *Zarathustra* is directed against democratic and socialist ideals. The *Übermensch* is the counter-image of the "last man," i.e., the functionary of the democratic-socialist society. This political meaning of *Zarathustra* becomes clear through Peter Gast's[48] explanatory text, which is conceived entirely from Nietzsche's world of ideas.

# 4. Culture and State. Hegel

A wise observer recently stated that the introductory sentences of *Untimely Meditations* opened up a "new intellectual-historical situation in Germany": here begins the opposition of the spirit, especially of the artistic spirit against the "Reich."[49] For many, Nietzsche gave the word "culture" a magical luster. Few definitions of the young Nietzsche were as fortunate as those of the first "untimely meditation": "Culture is the artistic unity in all expressions of the life of a people." Westphal drew the conclusion from this concept of culture that Nietzsche belonged to the sociologically, psychologically, and aesthetically oriented opposition of the Bismarckian Reich whose keyword was not "the state" but "society," an opposition whose spiritual leader is named Dilthey.[50]

---

48   "Peter Gast" was the pseudonym Nietzsche gave J. Heinrich Köselitz (d. 1918). The two were longtime friends. Köselitz collaborated with Elisabeth Förster-Nietzsche, the philosopher's sister, in the Nietzsche Archive, compiling the posthumous *The Will to Power*. [trans.]

49   Otto Westphal, *Feinde Bismarcks: Geistige Grundlagen der deutschen Opposition, 1848–1918* (Munich, 1930), 124.

50   Wilhelm Dilthey (d. 1911) was a German philosopher and historian who, perhaps most interestingly, developed a conception of three "typical" worldviews:

With psychology and art, it seems, Nietzsche also fought against the state and science; *for* culture, *against* the state — this was his motto.

But as far as Nietzsche is concerned, this construction does not correspond to the facts. The reasons for his opposition lie much deeper than an aesthetic motive reaches; the situation is much more complicated. It is precisely the social condition whose spirituality Westphal properly analyzes, precisely the psychological-aesthetic "culture" that Nietzsche has in mind when he says *culture*. Of course, he has another enemy in mind: the *national* and *Christian* state, of which Bismarck was the creator and leader of in his time. In order to properly see his relationship to this state, one must first know what the young Nietzsche actually meant by *culture*.

In fact, it seems as if opposition between Potsdam and Weimar[51] already existed when we read in the first "untimely meditation" that the victory of 1871 contained an immense danger: it could turn into a complete defeat — a defeat, even an extirpation, of the German spirit in favor of the "German Reich." Already here the Reich confronts us in those telltale quotation marks which subsequently always accompany the word when Nietzsche uses it. *Bravery* seems to him the most important characteristic of the German: steady and tenacious bravery in contrast to the pathetic and sudden impetuosity of the French. But this natural bravery and perseverance, plus strict war discipline, superiority of the leaders, unity and obedience among those led — this has nothing to do with culture. Breeding and obedience are something different from education; they also distinguished the Macedonian armies

---

1) *Naturalist* (wherein humans are determined by Nature); 2) *Subjective Idealist* (wherein humans see themselves as separate from Nature through their free will); 3) *Objective Idealist* (wherein humans see themselves in harmony with Nature). [trans.]

51  "… between Potsdam and Weimar …" — Potsdam represents traditional German conservatism (Prussian kings and Kaiser); Weimar represents liberal republicanism (of which the disastrous Weimar Republic was a manifestation). [trans.]

from the incomparably more educated Greek armies. So in 1871 we by no means won a victory over Roman culture — German reality is still styleless, we still have a false "educated-ness" [*Gebildetheit*] in place of real education, — a superficial culture of which the new work by D. F. Strauss,[52] to whom the attack of the first "untimely meditation" applies, is an example. There is no original German culture, we are still dependent on Paris in all ways, and it will be a long time before it can be said that we *were* barbarians.

The Macedonians are, of course, the Prussians, and the more educated Greeks correspond to the aesthetic Weimaraners; even the keyword "barbarians" is present. Anyone unfamiliar with Nietzsche must assume that he admires French culture. In truth, however, Nietzsche only wants to tell the Germans: *With the prevailing European cultural conditions, you will never get anywhere; here the French will always be ahead of you. You are destined for something else!* Taking Paris' side is the real Nietzschean challenge that emerges: the antithesis is meant *pedagogically.* The second "untimely meditation" provides us with proof of this: that superficial culture, which Nietzsche would like to bring to ruin, corresponds to a "decorative culture," i.e., a culture in which there is an "external" and an "internal," a form of life based on convention. For the young Nietzsche, however, this concept of culture is a Roman one; it is opposed to the Greek, according to which culture is "a new and improved physique" and means a unity among life, thinking, appearing, and willing.[53] The whole *decorative culture* — this is Nietzsche's saying — is ripe for destruction; his "untimely meditations" may help it fall; in no way do they want to recommend the Roman culture of the Germans as a model. The whole is measured against the Greek concept of culture.

---

52 David Friedrich Strauss (d. 1874) was a German (Protestant) theologian. His *Das Leben Jesu* (*The Life of Jesus*) caused a stir for denying the more mythical aspects of Jesus' life, focusing instead on a historical Jesus. [trans.]

53 See conclusion to the second essay of *Untimely Meditations.*

The contrast between Roman and German culture may come from Wagner, even the contrast between great opera and musical drama might be behind it: the depth the young Nietzsche gives to this contrast is new and completely unique. In him churns a dark and mighty vision of a German way of life, which is higher, richer, and more powerful than all previous forms. He has this future constitution of the Germans in mind when he speaks of the "German spirit," of an "education through art derived from the Germanic essence." He has everything but a state of society with high living culture, good theaters, and an artistically receptive audience in mind. Only from the notes in the *Nachlaß* do we learn what this actually means: "Culture is the artistic unity in all expressions of the life of a people." The objectionable and decisive word "artistic" is only understood if one feels its sharp point against science. Nietzsche understands the work of the scholar; he experiences daily the dangers inherent in the pure instinct for knowledge. He realizes: *pure knowledge, left to itself, drives to ruin.* It has proven impossible, he notes, to build a culture on science. The most ghastly thing is a "scholarly culture." *True culture has a unity that science cannot give.* Something must also tame science. Where else could the young Nietzsche seek this taming element than in art, to which he owes the highest moments of his life, whose greatest master, at the same time a true tamer of life, calls him a friend. "The taming of science now only happens through art." Adoration of art does not mean escape into the aesthetic or any idolatry of pure form, but the exact opposite: *it is a return to life.* In this sense, a strengthening of the aesthetic instinct appears to the young Nietzsche as "saving the German spirit." The turn to art is a turn to truthfulness and unity. "To be completely truthful — wonderful, heroic pleasure! ... Now art is getting a whole new dignity. The sciences, on the other hand, are downgraded a degree." In the above definition of *culture*, the emphasis is on the word *unity*. "The culture of a people reveals itself in the uniform control of the instincts of this people." At this point in the *Nachlaß*, we have a more correct definition.

When the young Nietzsche therefore speaks of art, he is not as far removed from the idea of the state as it seems, and it is no coincidence that the terms *tragic work of art*, *tragic person*, and *tragic state* appear near each other in the notes. *The Birth of Tragedy* is probably dedicated to an aesthetic problem; but the underlying cultural problem is anything but apolitical. It is only thanks to Nietzsche's friendship with Wagner that his thoughts about the Greeks have not taken on a different tendency. Because in the end, everything had to flow into Wagner's artistic endeavors — the friend was in danger! — the planned "Greek Book" was published in a purely aesthetic manner.[54] A large section on the Greek state had to be dropped. (There was certainly a deeper necessity in this, for the thoughts about the state would have been better connected with the fragmentary book on the pre-Socratic philosophers. Nietzsche recognized in the older Greek philosophy a philosophy of nothing but statesmen!) The Greek state undoubtedly played a formative role in the young Nietzsche's perspective. The tendency of the young friend of the Greeks is not to view the state in terms of the categories of an aesthetic culture, but, conversely, to view culture under the categories of the state. This tendency must have been all the stronger since the word of the enlightened Schlosser[55] continued to echo in the soul of the young Nietzsche, which he had heard in Burckhardt's[56] lectures: *power is inherently evil*. The origin of the state, according to the abovementioned fragment about the Greek state, is "terrible" — and yet hearts involuntarily swell towards "the magic of the nascent state." Even the subjugated no longer worry about such an

---

54   See my *Bachofen and Nietzsche*.

55   Friedrich Christoph Schlosser (d. 1861) was a German historian whose erudite and monumental *Weltgeschichte* (1815) had a lasting influence on continental academia. Nietzsche was likely familiar with his study of antiquity's culture (*Universalhistorische Übersicht der Geschichte der alten Welt und ihrer Kultur*, 1826). [trans.]

56   Jacob Burckhardt (d. 1897) was a Swiss historian and contemporary of Nietzsche. Art and culture were his primary interests. [trans.]

appalling origin; the state is fervently viewed as the goal and summit of the sacrifices and duties of the individual. One would think that devastated countries, destroyed cities, unruly people, and consuming national hatreds must forever remove us from the state. Nevertheless: "The state, of shameful birth, for most people an unending source of hardship, and often the all-consuming torch of the human race — and, yet, a simple sound makes us forget it all, a rallying battle cry inspiring heroic deeds, perhaps the highest and most venerable object for the blind and egotistical mass, which, even in the monstrous moments of state life, has the strange expression of greatness on its face!"

This passage is perhaps the strangest in Nietzsche's whole early work. It indicates that his thoughts could have taken the road to the state. *The Will to Power* would then not have been the work of a solitary man; moreover, a connection between Nietzsche's Heraclitism and the reality of the German state would have been within reach — Bismarck and Nietzsche would not have become enemies... One needs only imagine it to see this is not a question of possibility. It is precisely the unbridgeable abyss that we have to portray. Let us just keep in mind that Nietzsche does not belong to the "aesthetic-cultural" opposition of the new empire.

The young Nietzsche's concept of culture is characterized by the absence of any aesthetic or ethical hue. Genius — *enduring genius* — is the goal of all natural development and human effort. Everything else, including the state, is only part of the "necessary auxiliary mechanisms and preparations" for this ultimate goal. *Culture is where everything is subordinated to the creation and rule of genius.* Anyone who takes this thought out of the environment in which it has grown does not have a hard time inserting an anti-political aestheticism into it. But Nietzsche is *far* from an aesthetic concept of culture when he immediately cites slavery as the first prerequisite for his genius-state. So he has *real* Greek culture in mind, not a *dreamed-of* societal utopia. Culture, he says unequivocally, is not a people's choice; here inescapable powers rule, and these act as laws and limits to the individual. Savagery is also in culture's essence: begetting, life and murder are one; the blood-drenched winner is comparable to glorious Greek culture. What a barbaric, amoral, and genuinely Nietzschean image! The state is only a means to an end: it is the conqueror with the iron hand — but by this hand it leads "the wonderfully blossoming woman" of Greek society.

Art is the goal, and the way to this goal leads through the state. In the case of modern "cultural philosophers," this would mean: the reality of the state has to reshape itself according to the aesthetic goal until the condition corresponding to the "goal" is reached, i.e., until the state of an aesthetic-pacifist cultural community is achieved. For Nietzsche, the sentence has the opposite meaning: the reality of the state with all its horrors is the permanent prerequisite for the birth of the redeeming work of art. This hovers like a vision over the whole: if one takes away that reality, then this vision also disappears, which only arises from division and is only understood from opposition. The purpose of *The Birth of Tragedy* — Nietzsche's main aesthetic work — is to show this. Accordingly, Nietzsche states that the strength of the political instinct is a guarantee that the fertility of the soil from which individual geniuses can grow is not inhibited. At this point the educational idea that dominates the young Nietzsche comes in: so that the great work of art can arise again and again, the concentrated will of the state is required, which, "as a magical force," forces selfish individuals to make the sacrifices and preparations that a realization of great art presupposes. This includes "almost first of all" the education of the people.

Especially regarding the "only height of the sun in their art"[57] we have to imagine the Greeks as political people. Only the people of the Renaissance can be compared with the Greeks regarding this "unleashing of political instinct, such an unconditional sacrifice of all other interests in the service of this state instinct." The secret of the Greek concept of culture, and thus also of Nietzsche's, is the connection that exists between "state and art, political greed and artistic

---

57   This and the immediately subsequent quotations are fragments from an expanded version of *The Birth of Tragedy*. [trans.]

creation, battlefield and work of art." State and society are two sides of a single, comprehensive reality: the state is the "iron bracket" that forces the individual to serve the genius; it wages its wars, it robs and murders — but at the moment there is a standstill, when there are "some warmer days," the luminous flowers of genius sprout. So society as a cultural community does not replace the state, but society can only exist because there is a state.

The further features of what Nietzsche calls the secret doctrine of the connection between state and genius can only be hinted at: the original founder of the state is the military genius who creates the original state through separation and order. He immediately diminishes the significance of the family: the man lives in the state, the child grows up for the state and at the hand of the state. It is precisely through this that woman gains her effectiveness: as a being who is more closely related to Nature, as something that is eternally equal and at rest — the family means to the state what sleep means to man. It does not emerge, it lives as a mother in the dark because the political instinct, including its highest purpose, requires it. In more recent times, however, with the "complete disruption of the state tendency," the family has become a makeshift solution in place of the state, and accordingly the artistic aim of the state is immediately degraded to a domestic art. (Domestic music instead of tragedy!) At the same time, the rearing of the house is, as it were, the only natural one that tolerates questionable state interference with their rights — and rightly so, insofar as the modern state is mentioned.

Only now are we in a position to show the basic lines of Nietzsche's relationship to the Bismarckian state. We have seen that this relationship cannot be characterized as an opposition of the "spirit" to the warlike state, per the first "untimely meditation." It is neither by chance nor because of its timing that Nietzsche wrote of the "horrors and majesties of the war that just broke out"[58]; he sees in his problem a deep

---

58   That is, the Franco-Prussian War (1870–1871). *The Birth of Tragedy*, "Foreword to Richard Wagner." [trans.]

connection with the political events. Westphal assumed a disruption that should lie between this utterance and the beginning of the first "untimely meditation." We shall show that the basic idea remains the same not only between 1870 and 1873, but also afterwards.

The fragment about the Greek state, which together with "Homer's Contest"[59] and the fragment about the pre-Socratics, give Nietzsche's image of Greece a purer representation than *The Birth of Tragedy*, which contains a brief digression in its middle. Looking at the political world of the Hellenes, Nietzsche examines the present and identifies the familiar "atrophy of the political sphere, which is equally grave for art and society." What is the standard with which he approaches the present state? In the *Untimely Meditations* it is called "culture," and since one did not know how to interpret this word, one understood it aesthetically and believed that Nietzsche, as a "cultural critic," confronted the modern state. But it is the appearance of *war* that provides the measure for it. He differentiates between two concepts and conditions of the state: one in which war is an impossibility, and another in which the state is not based on the "fear of the war demon." The state in the first sense is to him a protective institution for *egotistical individuals*; the decision about war and peace is left here to the "egoism of the masses or their representatives," while in the other case it is entrusted to "individual rulers." Nietzsche therefore sees "the fear of war" in the "currently ruling nationalist movement" and the spread of voting rights. For him, nationalism, democracy, and pacifism form an *indissoluble unity*. In the background, however, he sees the *liberal-optimistic* view of the world, which has its roots in the French Revolution, "that is, in a completely *un-Germanic*, genuinely shallow Roman and unmetaphysical philosophy." But the really fearful are those "international, homeless money-hermits who, with their natural [rootless] lack of national instincts, have learned to abuse politics as a tool of the stock exchange and use the state and society as their own enrichment

---

59   *"Homers Wettkampf"* — an 1872 essay. [trans.]

apparatus. The only antidote to the diversion of the state-tendency to-wards the money-tendency, which the money-hermits fear, is war, war, and more war." The dangerous characteristic of the political present is therefore the use of revolutionary ideas in the service of a *selfish, root-less money-aristocracy*: *all evils can be traced back to this*, and "so I will be," concludes Nietzsche, "an occasional paean tuned in on the war."

A much more immediate political consequence from the thoughts presented here is drawn in the first version of the preface to *The Birth of Tragedy* to Richard Wagner. On 22 February 1871, Schopenhauer's birthday, Nietzsche wrote: *The only productive political power in Germany has now come to victory in the most monstrous way and from now on will dominate the German being right down to its atoms.* "This fact is of the utmost value, because something will perish in that power which we hate as the real opponent of any deeper philosophy and art." *That opponent is liberalism.*

> All that liberalism, built on a fanciful dignity of the human being, on the generic notion *human*, will bleed to death, along with its coarse brethren, from that rigid, previously indicated power; and we want to show the little charms and benignities clinging to it, if only this doctrine, which is actually *contrary to culture*, is removed from the path of genius. And what should that rigid power do — with its birth out of violence, conquest, and blood-shed, which has persisted for centuries — but prepare the way for genius?

Nietzsche hopes that Prussia's warlike power will bleed liberalism to death; on the other hand, he rejects the national state. We can guess his reasons for this if we read the notes: "The nationality principle is a barbaric brutality towards the city-state. This limitation shows the genius who gives nothing to the masses, but experiences more from the small than barbarians from the large." The state, as Rome exempli-fies, which cannot achieve its ultimate goal, swells unnaturally large; the world empire of the Romans is therefore nothing sublime when compared to Athens. But the unity of the nation is like the unity of a church: there are disadvantages connected with it. "Blessings of the fight," Nietzsche added. In Germany's unification he sees only a quantitative, not a qualitative change; for him it is the "unification of the German governments into one state." He must be an opponent of this union, because it only jeopardizes the goal of generating genius.

At the time of *Human, All Too Human*, Nietzsche vilifies nationalism: national dogma almost demands limitation: all higher culture can now — to their detriment — only become institutionalized. In the preliminary work on *The Will to Power* we find a rejection of "national hatred" and the remark that being *national* in the sense now (in the 1880s) demanded by public opinion, in more spiritual people there would be not only a slackness, but a dishonesty. Aphorism 748 of *The Will to Power* begins with a sigh about "this horned-cattle nationalism," behind which there is no thought. Nietzsche points to the mutual merging and pollination, in which the real value and meaning of the "current culture" lies, and sees the economic unification of Europe coming; as a reaction, the "Peace Party" [*Friedenspartei*] appears, which for a time was a party of the oppressed, but soon became the big party. The aphorism closes with the unfinished sentence: "A war party, with the same fundamentalism and severity against itself, proceeding in the opposite direction..."

At no point is the national state attacked for its inclination to wage war, but Nietzsche seems to hold onto his first view that democratic states must be war shy. The national state, however, is a democratic one because of its universal voting rights. In the abovementioned aphorism of *The Will to Power*, another contemptuous look falls towards the Bismarck Reich: "And the 'new Reich,' based again on the most worn-out and most despised idea: the equality of rights and voices."

So we come to the conclusion: *Nietzsche did not sympathize with the national movement that accompanied the founding of the Reich,*[60] just as he was uncomprehending and hostile to the "wars of freedom." If he finds only bad things in the national state, it is not because he

---

60  That is, the Second Reich, the Bismarckian Reich. [trans.]

looks at it through the eyes of a pacifist, but because he considers such a gigantic democratic structure to be incapable of preparing the people for the creation of genius. He expresses this rejection with great sharpness in the fragment on the Greek state, where the modern concept of nationality is ridiculed in the face of Pythia[61] and the Roman concept of the state is rejected with the words: it is an awkward wish to see a nation as a mechanical unit equipped with glorious government apparatus and military pomp.

We have shown that young Nietzsche is the *antithesis*: Spirit cannot represent against a power-state because it represents another by which it is excluded. It follows from this that, despite those introductory sentences of the first "untimely meditation," he is not on the side of art and education against the "Reich." He is not the representative of an aesthetic opposition, but is in opposition to a politicizing, aesthetic education. The philosopher of that "educated-ness" who thoughtlessly took part in the Reich's founding, that representative spirit of the German bourgeois intelligentsia, is Hegel. D. F. Strauss is not least dealt with as a Hegelian; the lectures on the future of our educational institutions are essentially against Hegel, for the Hegelian philosophy was fundamental for the new "general formation of the state." But when Nietzsche mocks the "apotheosis" of the state, he does not think of the warlike power-state, of which Hegel can also be seen as *the* theoretician, but with sound instinct he adopts the Hegelian total state as a cultural state. It is the state as a total concept, as it is developed in Hegel's *Philosophy of Right*, it is the spirit of Weimar, which is concretized into the state, that Nietzsche fights. Hegel is *the* thinker of the Classic era. He took advantage of the moment: his dialectic reflects the synthesis of Enlightenment and Romanticism he found in the time. The result was an image of the state as a moral organism that is at the same time an aesthetic whole, an idea of bourgeois society as a moral and aesthetic structure. Morality and aesthetics had entered into the

---

61    Pythia is the Oracle of Delphi. [trans.]

alliance that Schiller had demanded and the citizens of Weimar loved. As strongly as the young Nietzsche feels the personal greatness of Lessing and Schiller, he never listened for a moment to the bourgeois-liberal culture that was baptized in their names. In no phase of the development of this culture can he therefore be counted among an opposition which, with the help of the "spirit," opposed the state. It cannot be denied that Nietzsche's writings provided weapons to such an opposition. Nietzsche and his work, though, have nothing in common with it.

## 5. Bismarck. Against the Christian "Reich"

In Nietzsche's time, the leading stratum of the German bourgeoisie was *liberal* and *national*. National-liberalism, ideologically founded by Hegel, was the latest synthesis of Enlightenment and Romanticism and Nietzsche aimed to dissolve it. National-liberalism's intellectual failing lay in its unoriginality, in its "idealism." There was no bold new thought, there was no *realism*, there was no contact with what was really moving in the depths of the century. It was precisely this lack of realism that was bound to have a disastrous effect — because the nation believed it had just awakened to reality; it believed it made the transition from dreaming to "realpolitik" with success. In truth, there was only one practical-politician [*Realpolitiker*], which was the leading statesman; and there was one practical philosopher: the unknown Nietzsche. The question of the epoch was: will Bismarck have the strength to lead the German bourgeoisie out of national-liberalism, or will the same bourgeoisie, which had not the strength to create the Reich, later seize the gift that fell into its lap? What the *Untimely Meditations* sensed in 1873 later happened: the history of the Reich became a history of Bismarck's *spiritual defeat*. This process occurred right before the eyes, now opened in horror, of the other great realist: the merchant bourgeoisie became master of the statesman, liberalism and Romanticism took turns in politics — but above all, they made *good business.* The Reich flourished, but it was an *illusion*, and the philosophy that accompanied it ("moral idealism") was an illusion. During the World War,[62] the magnificent Roman-liberal structure collapsed, and, at the same time, the two great antagonists of the past became visible.

The documents in which Nietzsche's relationship with Bismarck is recorded are not easy to read. (The statesman took no notice of Nietzsche.) We have quite a number of passages throughout his works, as well as statements from letters and notes from the *Nachlaß* which mention Bismarck's name. He is also clearly suggested in some places where his name does not appear — for instance, everywhere we read "Reich" or "great politics" or simply "Germany." Just as the phrase "the artist" almost always refers to Wagner, "the statesman" always means Bismarck. Let us now explore how Nietzsche's relationship to Bismarck develops.

From a 16 February 1868 letter to von Gersdorff: "Bismarck gives me immense delight" — we can assume more *human* than *political* sympathy. While it was being printed, he deleted a passage from *The Birth of Tragedy* which mentioned the "leading statesman" of Germany and the "creative artistic genius" (Wagner) side by side. In January 1874, in connection with his criticism of Wagner, Nietzsche wrote the following: "Whether [Wagner] was right with the great trust he placed in Bismarck, the not-too-distant future will teach us." In *Human, All Too Human*, he deals with Bismarck under the following titles: "In Service of the Prince," "The Apparent Weathermakers of Politics," "New and Old Concept of Government," "The Helmsman of Passions," and "Leading Spirits and Their Tools." These sections more characterize than evaluate Bismarck, and there is something yet lurking in them. The aphorism "Consolation for Hypochondriacs" even speaks of *sympathy*. In between, however, appears — initially still in the form of the question — under the heading "Great Politics and Its Losses," an

---

62  World War I. [trans.]

aggressive tone: a people who are preparing to pursue great politics, lusting after political wreaths of glory, no longer belongs to their own cause as before; daily new questions and worries of public welfare devour its strength, and the question arises: is all this bloom and splendor of the whole *worth it*, if for this "coarse and colorfully iridescent flower of the nation, all the nobler, more delicate, more spiritual plants and shrubs" must be sacrificed?[63] Voiced here is a *fundamental aversion to democratic-nationalism*, the reasons for which we know. This aphorism is related to another of the same volume[64] in which the same objection is raised against the socialists. The socialists, it is said, desire to create a comfortable life for as many as possible. But if their utopia were really achieved, the soil from which the great intellect and the mighty individual grows would be destroyed by this life of well-being. The wise man must resist the "extravagant wishes of the unintelligent good" because in the perfect state there is room only for *exhausted individuals*. Nietzsche takes sides *against* Bismarck's direction as well as against his opposition, and his dissent is ultimately based on the *rejection of the democratic state*. One must always keep an eye on the two parallel actions — this is the only way to get an idea of the depth to which Nietzsche saw through the bourgeois society of his epoch. Strivings of the two opposing parties, the socialist and the nationalist, are characterized throughout Europe as "envy and indolence in different directions." "You are worthy of one another."[65] In the *Mixed Opinions and Maxims*[66] under the title "Subversive and Possessive Spirits" (§304) there is something yet valid today for the bourgeois culture of Europe. In a few sentences the new bourgeoisie, which differs from the socialists only in property, is characterized. "You must defeat yourself first if you want to win in any way over the opponents

---

63   *Human, All Too Human*, §481. [trans.]

64   "Genius and the Ideal State in Conflict," or §235.

65   *Human, All Too Human*, §480.

66   *Mixed Opinions and Maxims* was originally the second part of *Human, All Too Human*. [trans.]

of your prosperity." It is characteristic of Nietzsche's justice towards the two parties that the sharpest expression he used for nationalism ("national scabies of the heart and blood poisoning"[67]) can already be found here in connection with the other party: the widespread disease the "socialist scabies of the heart."

The subtlety and caution with which Nietzsche attacks can be seen from aphorisms 323 and 324 of the *Mixed Opinions and Maxims*. "To be a good German means to *de*-German" is the sentence with which the great attack on the "Reich" is initiated. The aggravation of the situation that occurs with this section consists in the fact that the "turn to the un-German" is thought to characterize the most capable of our men. The *aversion to the masses* no longer speaks here — tendentious malice does. The leading statesman, next to Wagner the only contemporary who is recognized by Nietzsche as an equal, appears to the ruling class more and more as the leader of the nation. This leader is a representative of the national principle — reason enough for Nietzsche not only to attack this principle as before, but to hit it even more finely and deeply. The truth is not important, we are in a fight! Incidentally, there are still means enough to tell the truth anyway, and after all, an author who counts on the best readers in Europe must not make it too easy for the smartest of them. The lone thinker competes with the most famous statesman on the same field; both are Germans — Germans of a kind that only come around every few centuries. For the real competitor, the *matter* is inseparable from the person: Nietzsche's genius consists to a large extent in taking the most *personal* so seriously that it becomes a "matter." He hits the leader of Germany, of the Germany that he, Nietzsche, was supposed to lead, right in the heart — if he is right: to be good German means to *de-German* oneself. Because the one who does nothing to de-Germanize, well, he *Germanizes* [*verdeutscht*] as much as he can. But that makes him un-German! With this he is moving away from our tradition, from the most capable of our people! So

---

67   *The Joyful Wisdom*, §277.

Bismarck is no longer one of the most capable of our people! Do not ignore the staid tone of the last words: they clearly show the double meaning of the aphorism. When did Nietzsche speak of "our people" in those years?

The immediately subsequent aphorism contains a witty critique of German weaknesses, under the guise of a foreigner speaking. Von Bismarck reveals here that Germany's greatest statesman does not believe in great statesmen. Bismarck is thus negated (he does not believe in himself) — this level of irony appears in the preceding aphorism and is intended quite seriously. This kind of hostility is not uncommon with Nietzsche.

Nietzsche speaks of Goethe's anti-nationalism with the strongest emphasis. (How wrong he is in this is shown by the wise man's wonderful conversation with Luden[68] on 13 December 1813.) If he wanted to expose Bismarck as the leader of the nation, he had to play Goethe off against him. That is why Goethe must be "an incident without consequences" in the history of the Germans — "who would be able, for example, to point out a hint of Goethe in German politics over the past seventy years!" And in the same book shortly before: "Just look at the best of our statesmen and artists: none of them had Goethe as an educator — they could not have."[69]

How consciously and carefully Nietzsche works can be seen from the following: It would be inconceivable that Bismarck is counted alongside Napoleon and Goethe in any of his published works — the latter belong strictly together as "Europeans" — Bismarck is on the *opposite* side. In the notes to the *Nachlaß*, however, Bismarck is mentioned no less than four times in the same sense as Napoleon; once he appears next to Goethe, and once, together with Frederick the Great,

---

68　Heinrich Luden (d. 1847) was a German historian with liberal (Rousseauian) leanings. [trans.]

69　*The Wanderer and His Shadow*, §125, 107 [*Wanderer* was originally the third part of *Human, All Too Human*. — translator]

above even Goethe. This is not about "contradictions," this is about a system.

Aphorism 167 of *The Dawn* puts beyond doubt that envy, the good Eris, and a competitive desire play a decisive role in this. This text is about the "Unconditional Homage." And who are the examples? The most widely read German philosopher: Schopenhauer; the most heard German musician: Wagner; and the most respected German statesman: Bismarck. The ranking next to Schopenhauer and Wagner says a lot — Nietzsche had no higher personal distinction to give. There are three times, he says, "a magnificent spectacle" can be seen, but one cannot agree on all three cases. Bismarck gets off worst: he doesn't even agree with himself! He is "a flexible spirit in the service of strong basic instincts, and for that very reason without basic principles." That would be nothing unusual about a statesman, but — one hears — "unfortunately, it has not been German at all so far"! Nietzsche as a eulogist of the German past, Nietzsche as an advocate of principles in politics, Nietzsche as someone who objects to a person because he has strong basic instincts — whoever does not notice the implication here cannot read. One has not yet read these books the way Nietzsche himself wished them read, here quoted from the preface: "*Read well* — that means read slowly, deeply, considerately and carefully, with ulterior motives, with the doors left open, with delicate fingers and eyes…"

But we are not done with the cited aphorism — it is a masterpiece of agonal malice. How much one would have to forget about these "three greats of the time," says Nietzsche at the end, in order to fully admire them in the future! It is more advisable to try something new, namely to become "honest," to learn that *unconditional homage* to people is something ridiculous, and that it is not about the *person* but about the *thing* that matters. This conclusion would be weak if it were only a question of the thought, for it is probably unfitting to say in view of three men revered by their nation: it is not the people that matter, but the things. But Nietzsche spoke this truth not in German, but in French. And the one from whom the sentence originates stands at the end like a statue made of ore opposite the false demigod [*Tagesgröße*] Bismarck: "This saying is like the one who spoke it: big, well-behaved, simple and silent — just like Carnot,[70] the soldier and republican. But is it allowed to speak of a Frenchman to a German, and a republican at that?" Who still doubts conscious art here: a Frenchman, a republican, a silent one — and there Bismarck, the German, the royalist, the man with the long parliamentary speeches![71]) Nietzsche uses the same "conscious art" in aphorism 95 of *The Joyful Wisdom*. In a section about Chamfort,[72] de Mirabeau[73] is introduced and — suddenly — it continues: "Mirabeau, who belongs to a completely different rank of greatness than even the first among the statesmanlike greats of yesterday and today." The punch line again lies in the fact that a Frenchman is being played off against Bismarck. Just as Nietzsche plays La Rochefoucauld against German philosophy, Bizet[74] against Wagner — as "ironic antitheses," as he writes to a musical friend in the case of Bizet — just as he thrusts Carnot and Mirabeau, completely random characters, against Bismarck.

Only in passing[75] is one characteristic of the Germans' education, which was exchanged for their political and national madness, and "which they no longer have," mentioned: this is direct failure for

---

70  Lazare Carnot (d. 1823) was a French polymath and military advisor under Napoleon. While more conservative than Robespierre, Carnot was a staunch advocate of the Revolution's principles, general egalitarianism, and republicanism. [trans.]

71  In *The Joyful Wisdom* (§104) it is said of Bismarck's speeches: there is an accent in them that the ear of a foreigner reluctantly rejects — "but the Germans endure it — they endure themselves."

72  Nicolas Chamfort (d. 1794) was a French aphorist. He was a member of the Jacobin Club. [trans.]

73  Honoré Gabriel Riqueti, Count of Mirabeau (d. 1791) was a prominent orator and leading figure of the Revolution's early days. [trans.]

74  Georges Bizet (d. 1875) was a French composer known for his opera *Carmen*. [trans.]

75  *The Dawn*, §190.

the person involved in the exchange. It is significant Nietzsche tries, because of Bismarck, to give the impression that the loss of that education was indeed a loss, but he simultaneously describes this education quite damningly: as presumptuous and harmless, as soft, benign, glittering idealism, and so on.

In *The Dawn*[76] the bitterness of failure is finally reached, which henceforth denotes the measure, or rather the immeasurability, in Nietzsche's relationship to Bismarck. A neutral line of thought about the future of the nobility is suddenly followed by the following words: "Last but not least: what should the nobility dabble with in the future when it seems from day to day it is becoming indecent to deal with politics?" Only when you apply the word to Bismarck does it make sense: it is a barb. And as if he were satisfied, Nietzsche adds a little further down[77] to Luther's verses, "Take our flesh, goods, honor, child, and woman: let go there — the Reich must stay with us!" and: "Yes! Yes! the 'Reich'!"

The mockery continues at the end of the great aphorism of *The Joyful Wisdom*,[78] which bears the title: "The Old Problem: What Is German?" Schopenhauer is praised here as a "good European," of course, not as a German, in whom everything attests to the *opposite* of pessimism: "Our brave politics, our happy patriotism, which decidedly enough bases all things on a little philosophical principle (*Deutschland, Deutschland über alles*)..." Is there a more grotesque comparison than the "happy" philosophy of Bismarck with the phrase *Deutschland, Deutschland über alles* on the one hand and Schopenhauer's pessimism on the other? If Nietzsche may otherwise have well-founded objections to Schopenhauer's pessimism, he may have just mentioned Schopenhauer, Wagner, and Bismarck together — here the old pessimist is good enough to be played off against the "Reich." Careless

---

76  §201.

77  §262.

78  §357.

readers then catalog such expressions under the heading "Nietzsche's Contradicting Position on Schopenhauer," while they belong under the heading: *Nietzsche's consistent struggle against Bismarck.*

As it were, "We Homeless Ones,"[79] at the end of *The Joyful Wisdom*, summarizes things nicely. It is dedicated to the opponents of Bismarck, the "Europeans of today," those homeless ones who cannot see a goal in "establishing a Reich of justice and unity on earth (because under any circumstances it would be a Reich of the deepest *mediocrity* and *Chinese-ism*)," nor can they speak of nationalism and racial hatred. These homeless ones live on mountains, *untimely*, in centuries past or to come, just so they can spare themselves the quiet rage to which they would know themselves condemned "as eyewitnesses of a politics that makes the German spirit desolate by making it vain, and which is a *small* politics besides." Nietzsche describes his own way of life here; he reveals why he cannot live in Germany. They do "small politics" there. But what does Nietzsche do? Apparently the opposite: *big politics.* "Big politics"[80] is the watchword of the following years in the fight against the "Reich."

In the terms "good Europeans" and "great politics" we see the weapons Nietzsche used in his final battle with Bismarck. This struggle is waged in the works of 1888 — everything once held back is now unleashed. Before the final battle, however, there is still a phase in which the old, indirect way of fighting takes place. The eighth part of *Beyond Good and Evil* is entitled "Peoples and Fatherlands." Its first aphorism (§240) is about Richard Wagner. This incomparable prose piece about the *Meistersinger* overture closes with the words: *The Germans are from the day before yesterday and from the day after tomorrow — they have no today.* Listen carefully! The existence of the Germany Nietzsche expelled is denied! Bismarck immediately followed Wagner; the aphorism dedicated to this is not inferior to the previous one in the art of

---

79  §377.

80  *Große Politik* — Baeumler here is highlighting Nietzsche's understanding of the utility of *groß*, which can be translated as *big* or *great*. [trans.]

*following.* Nietzsche cleverly divides the opposing opinions between two old men and thus reserves the possibility for himself to hover over the Bismarck problem and have the final word — you cannot defeat a rival more thoroughly... The overture's speaker appears to be defending German *small-townsfolkdom.* There is talk of the Germans' shyness and pleasure in community, of their foreignness and quiet boundlessness. And a statesman who *reversed* that, who narrowed the spirit of this people, made its taste national — *that would be great?* He may be strong, strong and great, but certainly not *big.* The whole aphorism actually has the concept of *magnitude* as its subject: the "*big* politics" to which Bismarck condemned his people is opposed to the "*big* thought" which gives greatness to an act and cause. It is a particular subtlety that Nietzsche does not name the statesman — he also does not name the one who brings the "big thought" — while Wagner is mentioned in the previous section without prejudice. Instead of the name there is a description of Bismarck that says it all in two words: "He who thinks and knows as much about philosophy as a farmer or *Korpsstudent*[81] is still innocent." Do you now understand what Bismarck is accused of? That he *overlooks* Nietzsche, that he believes he is *leading* the German people, while *next to him* the deepest, most revolutionary thoughts are being thought without his noticing anything. Nietzsche blames Bismarck personally for the fact that the Germans do not take him seriously, even though he has published work after work. Anyone who wanted to find this personal attitude towards Bismarck ridiculous would reveal that he only sees the whole thing in a moral-psychological way, not symbolically. Of course, Bismarck was not to blame for Nietzsche's ineffectiveness — but he was nevertheless guilty since the Reich he founded permitted the *bourgeoisie* to become *master* — the same bourgeoisie for whose best — Nietzsche's friends — the author of *Zarathustra* was only a fertile, but troubled mind. Franz Overbeck let

---

81  A "corps student" is a member of something like a fraternity. Historically, members would come from the upper classes and lean "conservative." The implication is that the indicted is inexperienced. [trans.]

his friendship with Treitschke[82] fall apart because of Nietzsche — and yet he did not understand anything of his friend's world-historical significance, as his notes shockingly show. In world history, Nietzsche was right when he made Bismarck and no other responsible for his own fate: the *big* man is symbolically, not morally liable.

"A stronger man becomes master of the strong," the aphorism concludes — what Christian consolation Nietzsche offers! And for the spiritual flattening of a people there is an adjustment — "the deepening of another."[83] It is not difficult to guess which other people are meant here — Nietzsche is explicit on this point.[84] In Germany the great statesman leads his followers right into the "unrest, emptiness, and noisy quarreling" of politics — in France, on the other hand, people of taste keep their ears shut "in front of the maddened stupidity and the noisy murmur of the democratic bourgeois." Despite a certain Germanization and *mobbing* of taste, the French were able to maintain their old cultural superiority over Europe. They are just a "halfway successful" synthesis of the North and the South and are therefore protected against the gruesome Nordic grey, against the German disease of taste, against "the excess of blood and iron, that is to say: *the 'great politics' which has been prescribed with great resolution* (according to a dangerous healing art, which teaches me to wait and wait, but not yet hope)." For the born *Mittelländler*, for the "good Europeans" (to whom Nietzsche counts himself here), an artist made music who discovered the "*South* in music": Bizet.

The episode of the "*South* in music" is spun a little further in the following aphorism (§255), but then the main line starts again (§256): the theme of France and Germany is brought to an end in the strangest way. Europe, Nietzsche begins, wants to become *one*. The politicians,

---

82   Heinrich von Treitschke (d. 1896) was a German historian and member of the Reichstag in Bismarck's Reich. He was a stalwart believer in the value of racial struggle. [trans.]

83   *Beyond Good and Evil*, §241. [trans.]

84   *Beyond Good and Evil*, §254.

of course, with "a quick glance and a quick hand," who are on top today with the help of nationality-madness, know nothing about it; their politics can therefore only be "intermediate-stage politics." All deeper and more receptive people of this century tentatively anticipate the Europeans of the future — only in weaker hours, in old age, for example, do they belong to the "fatherland." Examples are Napoleon, Goethe, Beethoven, Stendhal, Heine, Schopenhauer, and Wagner. The connection between Wagner and late French Romanticism is of particular interest. The German friends of Richard Wagner should consult with themselves whether his art did not come from sources and impulses beyond Germany, although Paris was of course indispensable for the development of his type.

Up to this point, Nietzsche has pushed the pretense, the antithesis — now he suddenly shifts and quite unexpectedly says something in honor of Richard Wagner's German nature. You have to read the passage: it negates everything that was said before; Suddenly everything is there again, which is Nietzsche's *actual* opinion. In everything, Wagner pushed it "stronger, harder, higher" than a Frenchman of the 19th century could ever do — thanks to the fact that *we Germans* are even closer to barbarism than the French. "Perhaps the strangest thing Richard Wagner has created is forever and not just for today inaccessible, incomprehensible, inimitable for the whole of the late Latin race: the figure of Siegfried, that very free man who is, in fact, far too free, too tough, too good-natured, too healthy, too anti-Catholic for the taste of old and frail civilized peoples." How *often* has Nietzsche's Romanism, his penchant for the South, his good Europeanism been cited[85]—but anyone who can write a sentence like the one above is only a very *ironic* admirer of *Frenchism* — for precisely this, that the Latin culture is old and crumbling, can only be felt by those who have the *youthful strength of the Germanic being.* Nietzsche's "Germanism" is

---

85   And it continues to be cited by all the vogue academicians, politicians, thespians, writers, etc. *ad nauseum.* Such incomplete interpretations do a disservice to Nietzsche, however. [trans.]

therefore not in the least weakened by his tendentious predilection for the South, for the Mediterranean taste of the Latin peoples. Freedom, hardness and audacity—the virtues that he places highest—still appear to him in the figure of .

The Siegfried idea is central to Nietzsche. We remember having met him above (pp. 66–69). Now he becomes a spear-point against the Romantics who one day find their way to Rome. The memory of the "anti-Roman Siegfried" is followed by the well-known *Parsifal* poem, which closes with the words: "Because what you hear is Rome—Rome's faith without words!" We know that in Nietzsche's view the Romans are closer to Christianity than the Germanic races—we know what that means for him. Then we have to measure what this conclusion of the main section wants to say about "Peoples and Fatherlands": it restores the balance in favor of the North.

In the spring of 1888 Nietzsche took on his last battle: it was against German culture, i.e., against Wagner, and against German politics, i.e., against Bismarck. In order to understand this last phase correctly, one must know the letters in which Nietzsche complains about the ineffectiveness of his existence. Since the publication of *Zarathustra*, he had been extremely sensitive to his "ineffectiveness" to trusted companions, who were quite silent. It was not his nature, it was the time—it was the intellectual narrowness of the German bourgeoisie that isolated him. As early as 1885 he wrote to his sister: "It is extremely horrible to be alone in such a way," and two years later he speaks to Overbeck of the "silent, now thousandfold loneliness." In 1886 we read in a letter to his sister: "It is hard, even downright crazy, that a person who is born for the richest and most extensive activity and could lay down and plant his best in selected souls, is condemned to make literature with his half-blind eyes—just to be able to work at all." His books are fishhooks to him (from the same letter): "If they don't catch a person for me, they have no point! … Get me a small group of people who want to hear and understand me—and I'm healthy!"

As early as the summer of 1882 it had become clear to him that it was Wagner who had "stolen all people from him whom it would make sense to work on in Germany." Now, in 1888, he is preparing to achieve what he had always hoped for: to become Wagner's heir. His attack on Wagner is said to grant him this inheritance by force. *The Wagner Case* is the first of the eruptions in the last year of his work. In it Nietzsche brings Wagner the war and "besides" (i.e., mainly) a German taste. Such falsehood as that of the Bayreuthers, as stated at the end of the brilliant little work, is no exception today. "We all know the unaesthetic concept of the Christian *Junker*, this innocence between opposites, this 'good conscience' in lies…" We must think of Bismarck here too. Numerous passages in his letters indicate that Wagner and Bismarck are only two names for the same obstacle. Nietzsche no longer wants to live in secret. He wants to *rule* Germany, he wants to stand next to Bismarck. "Even a member of the Reichstag and a supporter of Bismarck (Delbrück)," he wrote to Gast after Wagner's death, "is said to have expressed his extreme displeasure that I do not — live in Berlin, but in Santa Margherita!!" The letters to his friend Reinhart von Seydlitz above all make the situation clear: Nietzsche here — Bismarck there! "Between us … it is not impossible that I am the foremost philosopher of the age," he wrote, "maybe a little more, something decisive and fateful that stands between two millennia." And this world-historical consciousness confronts "our dear Germans"! In Germany, continues Nietzsche, there has not even been a single worthy review of his books. *Eccentric*, *pathological*, *psychiatric* are the terms used to describe them. Nobody protests, nobody feels offended when this philosopher is insulted. "Under these circumstances you have to live in Nice… With his own cynicism, God lets his sun shine more beautifully over us than over the so much more respectable Europe of Herr von Bismarck (who works with feverish virtue on his armaments and completely presents the aspect of an heroic hedgehog[86])." Also to von Seydlitz in the au-

---

86  A year earlier: "For this present Germany, as much as it stares into armaments like a hedgehog, I no longer have any respect. It represents the most stupid,

tumn of the same year of *Twilight of the Idols*: "I suggest in all modesty that the *spirit*, the so-called 'German *spirit*' went for a walk and lives somewhere in a summer resort — at least not in the 'Reich' — rather in Sils-Maria…"

Contrary to expectations, the section of the *Twilight of the Idols* that bears the title "What the Germans Lack" is rather restrained. The new Germany is even praised: it lacks the high culture necessary to become *master*, but it has "more masculine virtues" than any other country in Europe. Of course, one objection must be made: it pays dearly to come to power, for power gets *dumber*. Politics devours all seriousness for really intellectual things — "*Deutschland, Deutschland über alles*, I'm afraid that was the end of German philosophy." Bismarck devours everything, he *is* Germany. It is expressed with bloody scorn: "Are there German philosophers? Are there German poets? Are there good German books? — I am asked abroad. I blush, but with undaunted courage I answer: *Yes, Bismarck!* — If only I could admit which books one reads today… Damned instinct of *mediocrity!*"

It goes without saying that France should again receive high praise in this regard.

At the same moment when Germany emerges as a great power, France gains a new importance as a cultural power. Already today a lot of new seriousness, a lot of new passion of the spirit has moved to Paris; the question of *pessimism*, for example, the question of Wagner, almost all psychological and artistic questions are considered there incomparably more finely and thoroughly than in Germany — the Germans themselves are incapable of this kind of seriousness. — In the history of European culture, the rise of the 'Reich' means one thing above all else: a shift in emphasis. It is already known everywhere: in the main — and that remains the culture — the Germans are no longer considered.[87]

---

depraved, mendacious form of the 'German *spirit*' that has ever existed…"
87  *Twilight of the Idols*, "What the Germans Lack." [trans.]

With a precise chronological purpose it says in "Aphorisms and Arrows": "German spirit: a *contradictio in adjecto* for 18 years."[88]

Nietzsche expresses himself even more sharply in his last work *Nietzsche contra Wagner*: "Even now France is the seat of the most intellectual and refined culture in Europe and the highest school of taste: but you have to know how to find this 'France of taste.' The *Norddeutsche Allgemeine Zeitung*, for example, or whoever uses it as his mouthpiece, sees the French as 'barbarians' — for myself I am searching for the Black Continent, where 'the slaves' should be freed, near the North Germans..." The *Norddeutsche Allgemeine Zeitung*, the official organ of Bismarck, by "the slaves" we mean those who were following him, i.e., the Germans.

The German Spirit-German Reich antithesis completely dominated Nietzsche's late production. But this is not a theoretical antithesis, a contemplative statement, an assertion that would like to be true; it is a *weapon of war*. Competitive desire carries Nietzsche away. He leaves the realms of philosophy, he skips all thresholds: if Bismarck does not act, Nietzsche will. Nietzsche becomes a *politician*. The "great harvest time" has come: the draft of the main theoretical work, *The Will to Power*, is melted down into a new, vehemently polemical work of four books that will be entitled: *The Revaluation of All Values*. The first book is ready, it is called *The Antichrist*. *Twilight of the Idols* appears almost simultaneously. Nietzsche, in one of his last letters to Overbeck, spoke about them with terrifying clarity. One must read the whole passage:

> I take action against the Germans on this entire front: You will not have to complain about 'ambiguity.' This *irresponsible* race, which has all the great cultural mishaps on its conscience and in all decisive moments of history had something 'different' on its mind (the Reformation at the time of the Renaissance; Kantian philosophy, just as a scientific way thinking arose in England and France; 'wars of freedom' when Napoleon — the only

---

88  That is, *contradiction in terms*. "18 years" refers to the period spanning Germany's unification (under Bismarck) in 1871 to the 1889 writing of *Twilight of the Idols*, from which this maxim is taken (§23). [trans.]

one who was strong enough to form a political and economic whole out of Europe — appeared), today has 'the Reich' — this recrudescence of small states and cultural atomism are in mind at a moment when the great question of value is being asked for the first time. There has never been a more important moment in history: *but who would know?* The disparity emerging here is absolutely essential: at the moment when a rapturous and freeing spiritual passion takes possession of the highest problem of mankind and conjures up a fateful decision, such general *smallness* and *dullness* must stand out all the more sharply against it.

This is not enthusiasm: this is the clairvoyance of genius. Of course, this extreme wording only makes sense for those aware of the specific situation on which they are aimed. It is not about "humanity": it is hyperbole. It is about *Germany*. In all seriousness *Germany is at stake*: Nietzsche is planning a political attack on his fatherland. "We have to make the Germans mad with *esprit*..." (to Fuchs[89]). The word shows the direction of the attack: the Roman antithesis should have its say again — but it should not just be spoken. It is a deliberate betrayal when Nietzsche writes to Taine[90] in Paris: "I am unhappy to write German, although I write much better than any German ever wrote. In the end, the French will hear in the book (*Twilight of the Idols*) the deep sympathy they deserve, and in all my instincts I have declared war on Germany ('What the Germans Lack')." You must confront the matter squarely: Nietzsche specifically draws a Frenchman's attention to the section directed against the Germans. This is fundamentally different from sending the book in which this section is located: it is an act. Treason as an act is announced in the penultimate, still lucid, letter to Overbeck: "I myself am working on a *promemoria* [memorandum] for the European courts for the purpose of an anti-German league. I want to tie the 'Reich' into an iron shirt and provoke a war of desperation."

---

89   Carl Fuchs (d. 1922) was a music composer and critic. [trans.]

90   Hippolyte Taine (d. 1893) was a conservative French historian whom Nietzsche referred to as "the *first* of living historians" (*Beyond Good and Evil*, §254). [trans.]

What a poignant climax! He who was provoked by Bismarck into a war of desperation — he now wants to provoke the "Reich."

In the last weeks of his conscious life, Nietzsche was carried by a feeling of fate like never before. He repeatedly assured Overbeck that there was no longer any chance in his life. *Amor fati*[91] has always been his real religion — now he lives it. What does it mean to feel completely subject to fate? It means: becoming one with the power that appears in events; it means: removing the tension between yourself and the world. The personal becomes general, the general personal. Everything that happens is meaningful, symbolic, typical. There is no longer anything isolated: every *thing*, every *word*, every *person* has a mysterious relationship to our life and its ultimate goal.

Nietzsche's autobiography, which was given the title *Ecce Homo*, emerged from this heightened state. Shortly before the end, with the foreboding consciousness of this end, Nietzsche recounts his life. From this book written with fire glows the agony, the agony Nietzsche first experienced — to live as a man of world history in the sharpest light of consciousness, to have to know himself, his position in the context of things exactly, without having the power to change anything now, without even having the influence to convince those closest to him that "you" means a turning point in European history.

This has to be made clear: "Hear me! because I am this and that. Above all, do not confuse me with anyone else!" In a few words of the foreword (*Ecce Homo*) Nietzsche gives the shortest, most exhaustive characteristic of his thinking: "Error is cowardice." A warlike phrase. This is talk of one who sees himself as a warrior of the future combating a tired, late civilization approaching dissolution.

*Ecce Homo* is not actually an autobiography: it is a martial script in the form of a self-portrait. This is precisely what is demonic: the description of the most personal life automatically becomes *an attack on a whole world.*

---

91   That is, *love of fate* — one of the key concepts in Nietzsche's philosophy. [trans.]

Nietzsche immediately introduces himself "as the last anti-polit-ical German."[92] He believes that he is "more German" than current Germans — "mere Reich Germans" — are able to be. It goes without saying that he brings up the legend of his Polish ancestors, admittedly not without emphasizing the German core of his family. The whole text breathes a spirit of struggle against the "Reich"; it is only at the end, in the section dealing with *The Wagner Case*, that Nietzsche lets loose. He wants to tell the Germans "a few hard truths": they have commit-ted all the great cultural crimes for four centuries, and always for the same reason: "out of their innermost cowardice before reality, which is also cowardice before truth their untruthfulness, which has become instinct for them, out of 'idealism'…" They could never make up their minds, they always tried to remove and harmonize the contradictions. This neutrality and selflessness, "this lack of *party* [*Partei*] between opposites!" Everything *big* becomes *small* with them; they don't know what is big and small. "German" is an argument for them, *Deutschland, Deutschland über alles* — a principle, the Germanic peoples are the "moral world order."

But all of these attacks have a very personal connection. "And finally, why shouldn't I give my suspicions words? In my case, too, the Germans will again try everything to give birth to a mouse out of a tremendous fate. Up to now they have compromised themselves with me; I doubt they will make the future better. — Ah, if only I could be a false prophet here! My natural readers and listeners are already Russians, Scandinavians, and French — will this always be the case?"

What else is there to add to this revelation? Nietzsche does not want it to be as he says. He says the worst things you can say about Germany — *so you can hear him!* Germany is known as "Europe's lowland"[93]; you never get to the bottom of a German — *he doesn't have one*; the word *German* should be used as an international coin for *the*

---

92  *Ecce Homo*, "Why I Am So Wise."

93  *Twilight of the Idols*, "What the Germans Lack."

*will to be confused about oneself,* for this "psychological depravity." "At this moment, for example, the German Kaiser calls it his 'Christian duty' to free the slaves in Africa: among us other Europeans that would simply be called 'German'..." Nietzsche goes so far as to say that it is his ambition to be regarded as the *despiser* of the Germans *par excellence.* "The Germans are impossible for me. If I think of a kind of person who runs counter to all my instincts, it always turns into a German." For the Germans, every term depends on how mean they are: "But that is the superlative of meanness — they are not even ashamed to be *just Germans...*" One must always keep in mind that what we are dealing with here is the ability or inability of Germans to understand, to read, to appreciate. They have "no fingers for nuances, no *esprit* in their feet." In vain he searches for a sign of tact, of *délicatesse,* that he would have learned from Germans in his life. "From Jews, yes, never from Germans." Finally, he recalls that a foreigner, a Dane, first had fineness of instinct and courage enough to give lectures on his philosophy. Nietzsche knew this Dane, Georg Brandes, was a Jew. He was deeply averse to the Jews, in whom he saw the true priesthood; and even the flattering he drew from them could not change his mind. But just as he sets French culture against the German culture, so he also sets Jews against Germans. The antithesis is particularly sharp here because for him Judaism and Christianity are essentially one ("The Christian is the Jew once more"[94]). "The Jews are the priestly people of resentment *par excellence.*"[95]

We know: these are not Nietzsche's *actual* thoughts about the Germans, nor are they just exaggerations in the heat of the struggle. It is all said with deliberation. But what does Nietzsche actually think of the Germans? Why is he fighting against the "Reich," against Bismarck?

It must first be determined which qualities the German Nietzsche saw at all. He knew about the complexity and profundity, about the

---

94  *The Antichrist,* §44.

95  *Genealogy of Morals,* I, §16.

depth and extent of the German soul. Above all, he saw the contrasting characteristics of the German; he sensed the Germans' "diversity" very keenly. Above all else, however, he was certain of one thing: the Germans have not yet been exhausted, an enormous strength still sleeps in them. Everything around them is in decline (with the exception of Russia): Western culture is old, over-refined, skeptical, crumbling. The English are out of the question. But the Germans have not yet had a culture of their own. The young Nietzsche believed in this coming German culture; he fought for it, and never gave up his belief in it. We hear his *genuine* voice when we read his will to the Germans in *The Will to Power*:

> The Germans are nothing yet, *but they are becoming something*; this is why they don't yet have a culture — this is why they can't have a culture yet! — They are still nothing: that is, they are all sorts of things. They are *becoming* something: that is, they will soon stop being all kinds of things. The latter is just a wish, hardly a hope. Fortunately, it is a wish with which one can live, a matter of will, of work, of discipline, of cultivation, as good as a matter of indignation, desire, privation, discomfort — yes, bitterness; in short, *we Germans* want something from ourselves that no one yet wanted from us — we want something more!

> That this 'German as he is not yet' — has in him something better than today's German 'education'; that all 'becoming' must be angry when they perceive a contentment in this area, a brazen 'sitting down to rest' or 'perfuming themselves': that is my second proposition, about which I remain unchanged.[96]

Everything is here — it also says that hope can become a matter of unwillingness, discomfort, or even "bitterness."

From the beginning Nietzsche praised the Germans for their bravery. Will is still the least affected in the North; Germany has more masculine virtues than any country in Europe. But where there is still will, courage, and determination, there is still hope for the future.

---

96  §108.

"Those who can give orders will find those who obey: I am thinking, for example, of Napoleon and Bismarck."[97] There is also another side to German variety and ambiguity: there is a strong German kind. Handel, Leibniz, Goethe, and Bismarck are exemplars. "They lived harmlessly between opposites, full of that flexible strength that guards itself from convictions and doctrines by using one against the other and reserving freedom for themselves."[98] This kind is far from the inheritence of the Germans — theirs being the tendency to sentimentality, to false comfort, to darkness, and to that "quiet boundlessness" which Nietzsche praises in the Germans when he wants to make them *small*. Even Wagner and Schopenhauer, whom he likes to play off as "Europeans" against the Germans, should not be counted among them. "A good number of higher and better-equipped people will, I hope, finally have enough willpower to dismiss their bad taste for attitudes and sentimental darkness, and turn against Richard Wagner as much as against Schopenhauer. These Germans spoil us — they flatter our most dangerous qualities. A more vital future lies in preparation than in these rarer varieties of the race. We have not yet had any philosophers." It cannot be doubted that Nietzsche, in this note on the *Nachlaß*, regards his own philosophy as belonging to the same "stronger kind" of which he also counts Bismarck to be a representative.

This philosophy is "Dionysian," or, more correctly, *Heraclitic*. It is the philosophy of a person who either takes Christianity seriously — but then he can no longer be a European — or has to replace Christian values with new values. The Christian time has passed.

> Christianity is possible as the most private form of existence; it presupposes a detached, completely apolitical society — it belongs in the conventicle. A 'Christian state,' a 'Christian policy,' on the other hand, is a shameless *lie* — roughly like a Christian military leadership, which ultimately treats the 'God of Hosts' as *chief of staff*. Even the papacy has never been able

---

97  *The Will to Power*, §128.

98  *The Will to Power*, §884.

to pursue Christian politics…; and when reformers pursue politics — like
Luther — one knows they are the same Machiavels as any immoralists or
tyrants.[99]

Nietzsche believes that a German cannot really feel Christian. And
yet there lives next to him a German statesman of the "strong kind,"
who does not understand the world-historical opportunity, the immense task that now presents itself. There is much to praise about him:
he is "so far removed from German philosophy as a farmer or as a
*Korpsstudent*. Suspicious of scholars. That's what I like about him. He
threw away everything that stupid German education (with grammar
schools and universities) has wanted to teach. And he obviously loves a
good meal with strong wine more than German music: which is mostly
just a finer, woman-like hypocrisy and a disguise for the old German
man's tendency towards intoxication." In other places: he is not at all
comfortable, not naïve — and, thank God, he is not a German, "as
he says in the book"; he even understands parliamentarism as a new
means of doing what you want. But what is this statesman doing?

Nietzsche has two objections to make: Bismarck is not a Christian,
but he leads a "Christian" state; and Bismarck is handing Germany
over to the democratic movement.

The first reproach is as serious for Nietzsche as the second — and
both are essentially a single reproach. Already in *The Dawn* we find
an aphorism indicating how Nietzsche thinks about the Christian
Bismarck. "On the Deathbed of Christianity"[100] is the title of the few
sentences that one would have to consider insignificant and not in accordance with the weight of such a title if there was not a special meaning behind them. But the beginning is: "The truly active people are
now internally without Christianity…" Who else could Nietzsche have
counted among the "truly active" people of his time than Bismarck? It
is certainly no accident that in the same book in which the systematic

---

99   *The Will to Power*, §211.

100   §92.

attack on Christianity (i.e., on Christianity's "morality") begins, the planned attack on Bismarck is also opened. *The Dawn* reveals itself as the work in which Nietzsche begins to undermine Christian Germany, the "Reich." Behind everything Nietzsche does, and especially behind everything he does against Germany, stands his anti-Christianity. Up to now it has been thought that Nietzsche only gave theoretical expression to his position on Christianity. We have to retrain on this point. Nietzsche introduced a new way of philosophizing. His eminent literary talent enabled him to think and put his thoughts into practice at the same time. He is an "existential thinker," as Kierkegaard would put it — the inventor of a new kind of "practical philosophy"; he is one who always simultaneously does what he thinks. *He teaches an unchristian philosophy of struggle* — so by teaching it, he also struggles against Christianity. He not only fights against the concepts, but also against the contemporary powers that represent Christianity. Above these powers is the "Reich." That "royalism and Christianity" are combined in the leading statesman — *that* is his objection. "This nationality-neurosis and fatherland-foolishness are without magic for me: *Deutschland, Deutschland über alles* sounds painful in my ears, in truth because I want and wish more from the Germans than — your first statesman, in whose head the good ground of royalism and Christianity goes hand in hand with a ruthless politics of the moment and arouses my ironic curiosity." Nietzsche sees something reactionary in Bismarck's politics, in its "ancient trimmings," a remnant of the 19th century. He loathes this act-as-nothing-happened, this covert creeping past the real intellectual situation of Europe:

> Where did the last feeling of decency, of respect for oneself, go when our statesmen, an otherwise thoroughly unselfconscious bunch and antichrists-in-action, still call themselves Christians today and go to the Lord's Supper? … A young prince arrives at the top of his regiments, splendidly as an expression of the selfishness and arrogance of his people — but, *without any shame*, professing himself to be a Christian! … Whom does Christianity deny? What does it call 'the world'? That one is a soldier, that one is a judge,

that one is a patriot; that one defends oneself; that one's honor is respected; that one wants one's advantage; that one is proud...[101]

Only now do we understand the pointed words of *The Dawn*: it becomes indecent to deal with politics. Nietzsche associates this word "indecent" with a very specific meaning. Rome, the home of Western Christianity, is "the most indecent place on earth" for the poet of *Zarathustra*. In the above-cited section of *The Antichrist* there is the sentence: "What used to be just sick, today became *indecent* — it is indecent to be a Christian today." The word thus denotes a union of what cannot be united, an inwardly untrue connection: it is not fitting for Zarathustra to stay in Rome, nor is it fitting for a military leader or a statesman to live with Christian trappings.[102]

In summary: Nietzsche fights against the "Reich" — not because it is German, but because it is German and *Christian*. With its Christianity, Germany, for whom Nietzsche would like to provide spiritual guidance in Europe through his philosophy, is committed to those tendencies that are driving towards decline. In vain has he shown how corrosive Christianity is in its modern, dissolved form in all areas of life and spirit. He pointed out the disastrous consequences of the concepts of *equality* and *justice* — but the German spirit, which just now had the will to rule over Europe, the power to lead Europe, "under the pompous pretext of establishing a Reich, justified its transition to mediation, to democracy and 'modern ideas'..."[103] "Decadence reaches so deeply into the value-instincts of our politicians, our political parties: they instinctively prefer what *dissolves*, what accelerates the end."[104] The

---

101  *The Antichrist*, §38.

102  This, incidentally, is but one of the many criticisms the German philosopher Carl Schmitt levies against liberal-democratic systems: they are inherently *dishonest* — and such *indecency* will ultimately kill its host. [trans.]

103  *The Birth of Tragedy*, later "Preface."

104  Baeumler marks *The Antichrist* (§39) for this quotation, but I could not confirm it. Nietzsche, of course, makes many similar statements throughout his work, however. In keeping with *The Antichrist*, for example, we find the following

German Reich is but one of the "half measures" of modern democracy. In order for there to be institutions, there must be a kind of will,
instinct, imperative, *"anti-liberal* to the point of malice" — but instead
of the "will to tradition, to authority, to responsibility for centuries, to
the solidarity of gender roles forwards and backwards *in infinitum"* the
new Germany has the will to doom: *it is liberal.*

Nietzsche, as politician, has essentially only one concern: "the rise
of the democratic man and the resulting *dumbing down* of Europe
and the *diminution* of European people." He does not think nation-
ally because he ignores the national and democratic mass state. But
he thinks *German* in a new, bolder, and far-reaching way: Germany
should again become a leader in Europe. Of course, Nietzsche does
not mean this in the old "idealistic" sense. He does not want to make
Germany a nation of thinkers and poets again, he does not speak of a
kingdom of the German spirit or of a Christmas tree for the German
soul. Nietzsche knows that legalities and systems of power also belong to every spiritual rule. He does not want to make the Germans
apolitical; he does not want to found a German "cultural state" that
is the domain of good business and recreational trips of ironically
superior neighboring peoples, but wants to *lead the Germans to great
politics.* For this it is necessary they overcome their national compla-
cency, narrow-mindedness, and intellectual smallness: the dangers of
the nation-state. You have no reason to rest and relax. "If Germany
doesn't stand for something with more value than any other previous
power" — then it will only add to the heap of silly state-bureaucracies
in the world. "Can one be interested in this German Reich? Where

---

(§43): "Our politics is sick with [cowardice]! The aristocratic attitude of mind
has been undermined by *the lie of the equality of souls*; and if belief in the
'privileges of the majority' makes and will continue to make revolution — it is
*Christianity* ... and Christian valuations, which convert every revolution into a
carnival of carnage and crime! Christianity is a revolt of all creatures that creep
along the ground against everything that is *lofty*: it's the gospel of the 'lowly'
lowlifes..." [trans.]

is new thought? Is it just a new combination of power? All the worse if it doesn't know what it wants. *Peace and tolerance* is not a policy I respect. *To dominate* and *to help the highest thought to victory*—the only things that could interest me about Germany. What do I care if the Hohenzollerns exist or not?"

Nietzsche accuses the Bismarck era of failing to dissociate itself from the bourgeois-liberal conditions. "The era of Bismarck (*the era of German stupidity*). The exclusive interest that is now given in Germany to questions of power, commerce and exchange, and—last, but not least—the 'good life,' the rise of parliamentary *nonsense*, newspaper reading and literary participation by everyone about everything; the admiration of a statesman who knows and thinks about as much about philosophy as a farmer or *Korpsstudent.*" This description denotes the form of life that Nietzsche contradicts from his early youth, and at the same time his entire epoch is summarized from his own position: the Era of German Stupidity or the Era of Bismarck. With what *contempt* he described the bourgeois way of life in *The Dawn*, in *The Joyful Wisdom*, and in *Beyond Good and Evil*. He saw behind the morality of the modern "mercantile society," which is based on the principle: "Moral actions are actions of sympathy for others," a social instinct of fearfulness that wants life to be taken away from danger. Only actions aiming at a shared sense of societal security may be called "good."[105] Thus a "culture of traders" emerges, whose soul is as much *trading* as *personal competition* was for the culture of the early Greeks. In such a commercial culture the question of questions is: "Who and how many are consuming this?" Everything is valued according to the needs of the *consumer*, not the most personal needs of the *individual*. The trader knows how to assess everything without doing it; he constantly applies this appraisal, also to the products of the arts and sciences, of peoples

---

105 *The Dawn*, §174.

and parties.[106] But not understanding commerce is noble.[107] Typical of this culture are the modern meals, as they are already enjoyed today by scholars and bankers, after which one tries to expel the heaviness in the stomach and brain with exciting drinks. One wants to represent oneself well with meals like this. But only *money* is represented, because money is "power, fame, dignity, influence."[108]

Nietzsche sees "the meanest form of existence that has ever existed" in an "industrial culture" that is rank-ignorant and classless. The employee tries to sell himself as dearly as possible, but the employers lack "all those forms and emblems of a higher race that make people interesting in the first place." Nobility cannot be improvised. The "vulgarity of industrialists with red, fat hands" gives the common man the idea that only chance and luck have raised one above the other here. "Well, so he concludes, let's try chance and luck! Let's throw the dice! — *and so socialism begins*."[109] The book in which these sentences appear was published in 1882. One must always keep an eye on the impartiality and sharpness of this description if one is to correctly assess Nietzsche's relationship to Bismarck. The philosopher saw what the statesman did not: the actual justification of the socialist movement, which is based on the fact that the ruling class is in fact in possession of power, i.e., in possession of money, but in reality no longer rules — because domination includes a superiority that finds its natural expression in the "noble form." But what *bourgeois society* calls "noble," Nietzsche rightly considered another expression of *plebeianism*. He foresaw the overthrow of a ruling class that busied itself with external appearances and not internal character, and in this respect, Nietzsche was infinitely superior to Bismarck.

---

106 *The Dawn*, §175.

107 *The Dawn*, §308.

108 *The Dawn*, §208.

109 *The Joyful Wisdom*, §40.

The aphorism goes even further. Nietzsche is not fooled by the militarism of the Reich: he sees that the industrial spirit is much stronger than the military spirit. This is precisely the reason for the lack of noblity. "Soldiers and leaders still have a far loftier attitude towards one another than workers and employers. For the time being, at least all military-based culture still ranks high above all so-called industrial culture." Submission to powerful, dreadful, even terrible persons, to tyrants and military leaders is by no means as distressing as "submission to unknown and uninteresting persons, as are all greats in industry: in the employer the worker usually sees only a cunning, parasitic hound of people speculating on every need — whose name, shape, custom, and reputation are completely inconsequential to him." In this *impersonality*, we add, Nietzsche sees the real cause of the evil, because this relationship necessarily lacks responsibility. Every personal relationship, even that of the tyrant to the subjugated, is higher because the tyrant is personally liable for what he does. Tyrannicide is an expression of this liability. A class that has power in the form of money rules irresponsibly in every case: nobody is to blame for what happens, because *behind the impersonal system, the individual disappears*. The employer may be a harmless Christian and family man in his private life, feeling completely innocent. Nobody thinks of murdering him — and yet the presence of these more or less innocent people weighs down like doom over the whole and creates that dull pressure, that atmospheric gloom, which is an expression of the internal crisis. *With what scorn* would Nietzsche have responded to the attempt to alleviate this situation by demanding — without addressing the problem's source — a "sense of social responsibility" from the donors and entrepreneurs!

If modern bourgeois society is based on the instinct of fearfulness, then the need for security and peace must necessarily grow and ultimately lead to a state in which war is ended and morally outlawed. The culture of industrial society ends in pacifism. Nietzsche also foresaw this development; he has already identified it as a general tendency in the "Reich" (which actually later proved to be incapable of leading a war politically). This is why he never tired of pointing out the necessity and importance of wars in *Human, All Too Human*. Such thoughts all stem directly from his views on state and culture laid down in the fragment on the Greek state. War is essential. "It is vain rapture and prettiness to expect much from mankind when it has forgotten how to wage war." The raw energy of the encampment, the concerted and organized destruction of the enemy, the proud indifference to casualties and to one's own existence cannot "for the time being" be communicated to souls by anything other than great wars. Even in the perilous voyages of discovery and scientific expeditions the desire for adventure and danger is expressed. A highly cultivated and therefore necessarily dull humanity *needs temporary relapses into barbarism in order not to forfeit its culture and its very existence through the means of civilization.*[110] In times of security, life is stagnant. The secret to reaping the greatest fertility and the greatest enjoyment of existence is: *live dangerously!* "I welcome all signs that a more masculine, warlike age is dawning, which above all will bring bravery to honor again!" Heroism must be carried into the knowledge that wars must be waged "for the sake of ideas and their consequences."[111]

This is where the concept of *great politics* arises: What drives great politics forward is the need for a feeling of power, which from time to time emerges from inexhaustible sources not only in the souls of the individual but also in the lower strata of the people. The hour always comes when the masses are ready to add to it their life, their resources, their conscience, and their virtue. Then the pathetic language of virtue is spoken. "Wonderful madness of moral judgments! When a person feels power, he feels and calls himself good: and it is precisely then that

---

110 *Human, All Too Human*, §477.

111 *The Joyful Wisdom*, §283.

the others, on whom he has to unchain his power, call and feel him evil!"[112]

There is only one antidote to the increasing assimilation, mollification, and diminution of European people: *danger and war*. Nietzsche likes to take the word *war* to mean *struggle* generally. He is too far removed from valuing life for life's sake and too hostile to the moral, humanitarian ideology Christianity generates to counteract real wars between peoples. For him, pacifism is an ideal of the herd animal: it is a form of *slave-morality*. Since real wars include the peoples and states that wage them, but Nietzsche denies the national, democratic mass state because of its leveling tendency, we find passages in his work like the one cited above to justify the wars of nations. At the same time we see how he shifts the emphasis ever to the *spiritual struggle* for power. This struggle for supremacy is now waged in Europe. Should this result in bloody wars, Nietzsche does not shrink from justifying them.

Europe is in a struggle of the greatest thought, of "power" — so culminates Nietzsche's political vision. European man now strives toward the condition represented in *Zarathustra*'s "last man." The *Übermensch* is the formula for overcoming this condition. The *Übermensch* will liberate the world from the "last man," i.e., from the ultimate result of Christian-democratic development. "Wrestling for the use of the power that represents humanity. Zarathustra calls for this wrestling." The "revaluation of all values" will initiate the fight. In *Ecce Homo*, Nietzsche's final and actual goal is expressed thusly: "The concept *politics* is completely elevated to the realm of *spiritual struggle*. All power structures of the old society were exploded — they all rest on a lie: there will be wars the likes of which have never been seen on earth. It is only from me onwards that great politics will exist on earth."[113]

"May Europe," we read in a *Nachlaß* note from the time of *The Will to Power*, "soon produce a great statesman, and he who is now, in this

---

112 *The Dawn*, §189.

113 *Ecce Homo*, "Why I Am A Fate."

*small* age of plebeian myopia, hailed as 'the great realist,' there stand *small*."

The contest is over. Nietzsche is victorious.

# 6. The Good European

Something remains to be said of the "good European." In order to be able to determine the value of this term, it is best to start from the most representative place it appears: the preface to *Beyond Good and Evil*. In Europe there is now "a magnificent tension of the spirit, such as was not on earth before: with such tension, one can now aim at the most distant goals." Of course, European people perceive it as a crisis, and two attempts have already been made to draw the bow: once through Jesuitism, and the second time through the democratic Enlightenment with the help of freedom of the press and newspaper reading. The Germans, it is said at the end, invented gunpowder — all due respect! — but they made things square again: they invented the printing press. "But we," continues Nietzsche, "who are neither Jesuits nor democrats nor even sufficiently Germans, we good Europeans, and free, very free spirits — we have it still, all the distress of spirit and the tension of its bow! And perhaps also the arrow, the task, and, who knows? *the goal, too…*" With the "bow" Nietzsche alludes to the struggle for Europe. The antithesis is clear: "good European" is the opposite of a person who is *only* German. The good European is a *libre penseur* [free thinker], a free spirit, and therefore well-disposed towards French, a lover of the Romance cultures, a friend of the Mediterranean and "music of the South." Good Europeans include all spirits who understand form, artistry and psychology, people who have a sense for nuance, scornful, superior spirits who live homeless on high mountains. Occasionally Schopenhauer and Wagner also belong to them — of course, never Bismarck or other Germans. We have seen how quickly Nietzsche drops the term when it comes down to it: it is not attached to a being, to a substance; it only has a function, a purpose — the purpose of offending Germans and a kind of sphere around it to create the lonely one who is not recognized by them.

The concept of the "good European" first appears in *Human, All Too Human*,[114] which from the text the "annihilation of nations" is (wrongly) concluded. The good European to whom the German should be particularly suitable due to his talent as an interpreter and mediator is considered the European of the future. In *The Wanderer and His Shadow*,[115] every "good European" is expected to learn to write well and increasingly better: it helps nothing, adds Nietzsche, "even if he was born in Germany, where bad writing is treated as a national privilege." The real purpose of this is to set the conditions, no matter how distant, "where the great task falls into the hands of the good Europeans: the management and supervision of the entire earth culture." Whoever is against good writing and good reading reveals how to become more *national*[116] since he hinders understanding and is, consequently, "an enemy of good Europeans, an enemy of free spirits." In rejecting national differences, Nietzsche goes so far in *The Wanderer* that he pits fashion as something *European* against national dress.[117] This train of thought reaches its conclusion later in the same work, wherein the "victory of democracy" is predicted.[118] The provisional result of rampant democratization will be "a European League of Nations in which every people, delimited according to geographical expediency, has the position of a canton and its special rights."

The "good European," as he appears in these sections, is evidently identical to what Nietzsche calls the "last man" in *Zarathustra* and the "future European" in *The Will to Power*: he is the product of democratic leveling — "the most intelligent slave-animal, very hardworking, very

---

114  §475.

115  §87.

116  In the Bismarckian sense. [trans.]

117  §215.

118  §292.

modest, excessively curious, pampered, and weak-willed, with cosmopolitan passions and an *intelligence-chaos [Intelligenzenchaos]*."[119] It is undoubtedly *not* the "good European" that Nietzsche means when he says in *Ecce Homo*: "It takes me no effort to be a 'good European.'"[120] The good European in this latter sense is undoubtedly that free spirit who belongs to a small elite of Europeans.

However, there is also a third concept of the "good European." This latter is no longer a free spirit, but a warlike spirit. Far from being an enlightener for whom the spread of good reading and crediting is important, he is fighting *against* the Age of Enlightenment, in which people knew how to read and write so well: "Essentially, we *good Europeans* are waging war against the eighteenth century."[121] These good Europeans are detailed in *The Will to Power*: they are the people of Nietzsche's philosophy. They are "the lawmakers of the future, the masters of the earth."[122] A *Nachlaß* passage reads: "Principle — 1. Create a species of beings to replace the priest, teacher, and doctor; 2. Institute a *spiritual* and *physical aristocracy* that breeds new strength into itself to counter the democratic world of the *failed* and *lame*.[123] For this type we also find the name of the "higher European," who is called a forerunner of great politics.[124] It is this "higher European" whom Nietzsche addresses in September 1886 at the end of the preface to the second volume of *Human, All Too Human*: "You, whose consolation it is to know the way to a new health, ah! And to go — a health of tomorrow and the day after tomorrow, you predestined, you victorious, you time conquerors, you healthiest, you strongest, you good Europeans!"

---

119  *The Will to Power*, §868.

120  "Why I Am So Wise."

121  *The Will to Power*, §117.

122  §132.

123  "The Lords of the Earth."

124  *The Will to Power*, §463.

# Epilogue

PERHAPS IT WOULD BE in keeping with Nietzsche if one were to say: the rule of the spirit is another term for *anarchy*. That Nietzsche could be considered a politicizing "spirit" is one of the ironies of history. The error is ultimately based on Nietzsche's disproportionate focus on the state and the legend of his "individualism," which is difficult to eradicate. In his world, the individual always seems to be right in relation to the race, the people, and the state. It should be surprising that the individual rises above the others — Nietzsche's world, then, cannot be completely unrelated to the state. But the state-individual relationship is buried: nowhere is his era felt as strongly as here. The fact that politics is in the background for Nietzsche is not predicated on the matter at hand. In the *Politeia*[1] of his great opponent Plato it says, "The greatest punishment is to be ruled by someone worse if one does not make the decision to rule oneself." This state-founding maxim could stand above *The Will to Power* as a motto. To prevent the worse from reigning because the better stand aside out of disgust — this is undoubtedly one of Nietzsche's goals.

Nothing seems more difficult than finding the transition from the individual to the collective in Nietzsche's world. And yet the collective necessarily lies on the path followed by "the guidelines of the living body." The philosopher of the *will to power* clearly heard that faint rustling of the current flowing under the ages from which the individual emerges. The conscious connections made by people through time

---

1   That is, Plato's *Republic*. [trans.]

are usually thought to be the most important — "while the fundamentally true connection, through procreation, goes its unknown way."[2] The individual is just a *fallacy*: "We are more than the individual: we are the whole chain, with the duties of all conceivable futures in the chain."[3] "The isolation of the individual should not mislead — in truth, something flows beneath the individuals."[4] Whoever thinks about the guidelines of the living body cannot be an individualist — just as little as one who thinks historically can be an individualist. There is a temporal break in Nietzsche's relationship to the great commonalities as well as in his relationship to history. How little he thought *individualistically* within the historical realm is proven in *Genealogy of Morals*: not individuals, but genders, races, peoples, classes [*Stände*], and the contrasts between them — the pathos of distance — are for him the starting points of all historical existence. Sometimes it looks like he is only interested in the "future of humanity." But the realist knows too well that there is no such thing as a "human species" as an historical unit. The collective from which the individual person originates is never "humanity," but always a concrete unit: a *race*, a *people*, a *class* [*Stand*]. "Preservation of the *community* (of the *people*) is my correction — instead of 'preservation of the species.'" "The various moral judgments have so far not been traced back to the existence of the species 'man': but to the existence of 'peoples,' 'races,' etc. — namely, of peoples who wanted to assert themselves against other peoples, of higher ranks that wanted to sharply distinguish themselves from the lower ranks."

Accepting the demands of a people strengthens the individual; by participating in the tensions that exist between the units of world history, he is walking the path to greatness. For all active natures, this path leads through the state. There is no doctrine of the state in

---

2     *The Will to Power*, §676.

3     *The Will to Power*, §687.

4     *The Will to Power*, §686.

Nietzsche's work — but his work has opened up all the ways to a *new* doctrine of the state. How should the philosopher who understands the living body as a "structure of government" *not* be a teacher of the state? "As little state as possible!" This call of disgust was aimed at the Roman-Christian form of decay of the state, not the political way of life. The *Nachlaß* contains a passage about the state that allows one to guess what Nietzsche could have taught about it in a different era:

> Heroic impulses — not purdence — were the driving forces in the state's development: the belief that *there is something higher than the sovereignty of the individual.* There is reverence for the gender and the elders of the gender: the younger makes his sacrifice to him. Reverence for the dead and the traditional laws of the ancestors: to them the living brings his sacrifice. Homage to someone who is spiritually superior and victorious is at work: the delight of meeting his paragon in person: *this is where vows of loyalty arise.*

> It is not coercion or cleverness that upholds the older forms of government: *it is the flow of noble impulses.* Coercion would not be able to be exercised at all, and cleverness is perhaps still not individually developed enough. A common threat may be a cause for coming together, and there is something enraputuring about the feeling of new common power and noble resolve.

The state as an *heroic* phenomenon, as a system of rule, as a source of all great things, as a means and expression of the struggle for the highest power, which is *never* merely physical or economic — *that* is a *Germanic* conception of the state. This conception is alive in Nietzsche, even precisely where he speaks *against* the state, and precisely where he attacks Germany. This conception is also alive in Hölderlin's[5] hymns. Where there is no *struggle for a supreme form,* there can be no state. In the German Kaiser's Italian campaigns lives the state-spirit of which the Teuton is capable. This state-spirit does not aim to secure power

---

5    Johann Christian Friedrich Hölderlin (d. 1843) was perhaps *the* German poet. In some respects he presages Nietzsche [trans.]:
     *Whoever works with his whole soul never errs,*
     *He needn't split hairs, for no power can stand against him.*

economically and financially — it has a dangerous contempt for all such static thinking — it is purely dynamic: *the state exists where there is greatness, where a bold leader commands valiant men and pursues far-reaching goals.* There is a state where there is courage and pride, boldness and strength, where purpose and tasks beckon. In the youth of the European peoples, the heroic idea of the Germanic state made a tremendous impression; neighboring kings have voluntarily bowed to the Saxon, Salian and Swabian emperors. This has been over since the 13th century — the grand century of the Church — and the collapse is so deep that not even in Germany has memory of the heroic days been preserved.

Nietzsche recalls this memory in us. His attack on the "Reich" arises from the feeling of the world-historical task that awaits us. He did not want to know anything about the state as an Hegelian moral organism, but neither did he want to know anything about Bismarck's Little Christian Germany. Before him stood the old task of our race: the task of being the leader of Europe. German politics in the future is unthinkable without an element of Hölderlin and Nietzsche: the future of Europe depends on Germany's youth. The state is not a problem for the youth of the other European peoples; for the German youth, it is the problem. What would Europe be without the Germanic North, what would Europe be without Germany? *A Roman colony.* How correctly did our enemies perceive the Germanic in Nietzsche during the World War. They saw his work as an assassination attempt on "Christian culture," i.e., on a well-established combination of *gospel* and *business*; they felt this honest and courageous spirit as the negation of that civilization that was waging war under the sign of the cross, they felt the Siegfried-attack on the urbanity of the West. The irreconcilable *opponent* of the Western *civilization* that declared war on us in 1914 — *that* is Nietzsche. Because this civilization is the Christian-Roman "Occident," whose illusions he destroyed in *The Will to Power*. Over the millennia, the spirit of the North — foreign to Rome and related to Greece — has regenerated in him. For him, the Christian-Germanic state of the Romantics and the "practical-politicians" [*Realpolitiker*] is just as much a deviation from the spirit of the North as the *civilizing welfare-state of the West*. He occasionally hints at a foreign policy that points radically to the east. In Russia he sees an enduring power — one that can wait and promises something more. "Russia — the opposite of the wretched European *small* states and skittishness, which entered a critical state with the establishment of the German Reich… The whole West no longer has those instincts from which *institutions* grow, from which the *future* grows…"[6] Nietzsche sees the entry of Russians into culture as one of the signs of the next century: "A grandiose goal. Proximity of barbarism, awakening of the arts, generosity of youth and fantastic madness and real *willpower*." These words were spoken at a time when there was no Soviet Russia — can one imagine a better anticipation of its essence than is contained in these lines? And there is a clearer rejection of Western politics: "We broke an unconditional union with Russia, and with a new joint program which would not allow any English schemes to reign in Russia. No American future!"

Against the backdrop of world history, Germany can only exist under the form of greatness. It only has the choice of being or not being the *anti-Roman* power of Europe. If it fits into the civilization of the West, it submits to Rome; if it forgets its Germanic origins, it falls for the East. The creator of a Europe that is more than a Roman colony can only be Nordic Germany, the Germany of Hölderlin and Nietzsche. Nietzsche does not belong next to Bismarck, he belongs to the age of the Great War. The German state of the future will not be a continuation of Bismarck's creation, but will be forged out of the spirit of Nietzsche and the spirit of the Great War.

---

6    *Twilight of the Idols*, "Prowlings," §39.

# Appendix

## Nietzsche and National Socialism[1]

I F THE GERMAN REVOLUTION[2] were a process only within the German bourgeoisie, if this revolution were just a revision of existing concepts — then the subject of "Nietzsche and National Socialism" would have no deeper meaning. But the "and" of this title does not mean that any thoughts of Nietzsche are to be brought into a more or less close connection with any thoughts of National Socialism; rather, this "and" indicates a deeper relationship between the two. Nietzsche lived isolated from and imagined himself outside the German bourgeoisie and, from his extreme position, fought against the bourgeois state as a whole. The National Socialist movement, too, was created from a location outside the bourgeois world. It did not arise within the German bourgeoisie and its traditions, but as the creation of a *single man* who was decisively shaped through his own political experience and through the Great War.

National Socialism, in its origins, hardly drew directly from Nietzsche. In the first years after the war nobody thought of relating the new movement to Nietzsche. At that time only a few suspected what the German people's awakening, which began on 1 August 1914,

---

1     This essay, written in 1934, is excerpted from Baeumler's *Studies in German Intellectual History* (1937). [trans.]

2     That is, the National Socialist revolution (1933), of which Hitler's ascension to Chancellor was the culmination. [trans.]

actually meant. It was only the 1933 revolution that opened many eyes to the fact that a new order was dawning. As it is with the peaks of high mountains, so it is with the Great War: it is distance that brings clarity. But anyone who sees the Great War has seen both Nietzsche *and* National Socialism. Because from the fire and blood of the Great War, National Socialism was born — it points backwards to the mighty community of deeds and sacrifices of our people, to the greatest event in our history. Nietzsche, however, points forward to this event from his time. He is the only one of his age in Germany who felt the ground tremble and saw the coming catastrophe. He predicted Nihilism, "the scariest of all guests"; he predicted the state of confusion, disbelief, the devaluation of all values, the disintegration of all forms of life with the certainty of a seer. He recognized modern democracy as the historical form of the decline of the state; he described the traits of modern man with inexorable sharpness — all those characteristics which stood in the way of Hitler's victory for years: first and foremost the *neutrality* of the educated, the *opportunism* of the ruling class and their need for peace and security, the *alienation* of German people from Nature and the tasks of history. The lack of "political leadership" during the World War meant nothing more than the withdrawal of the German bourgeoisie from world history.

Nietzsche's contemporaries, even his friends, saw him as an eccentric person, if not a madman, simply because he *resisted* everything that *claimed* validity at the time. He was the critic, the denier, he lacked a "positive program"! This same accusation was incessantly thrown against the National Socialist movement. It is the typical expression for the chasm that separates the great doers, the anticipatory, who want the impossible, from those who only consider the possible. It was so hard to believe that this Weimar Republic, this *constitution*, this civic order *based on defeat* and on the lack of any will to overcome defeat — that none of this should mean anything, while it indeed showed its factuality in the form of bans, dismissals, arrests, and rubber truncheons. And yet it was *decisive* that there existed a man who declared all of this hollow and void. This man could not predict what would be in a year's time — no man has ever been able to do that — but he yet knew: *all this is ripe for destruction* — and what falls should still be pushed.

If we transfer Hitler's position on the Weimar Republic to a solitary thinker of the 19th century, then we have Nietzsche. In declaring war on the Weimar Republic, Hitler declared war on a development spanning centuries, even millennia. While Nietzsche criticized the education, culture, and politics of his century, he also began the struggle against the development of millennia. There may yet be people who see Hitler only as the liquidator of Weimar — but his great significance is as little exhausted in this as is Nietzsche's in the liquidation of the 19th century. Both stand at crucial points in that most important movement in our history, which we can call the "Nordic Movement." On the political line of this movement stand the great kings of the early Middle Ages, stand the foundations of Prussia, stand Bismarck and Hitler. On the religious-spiritual line of this *Ghibelline* movement[3] stands Germanic paganism, Eckhart, Luther, and Nietzsche.

Nietzsche and National Socialism, then, stand beyond the traditions of the German bourgeoisie — what does this mean? The spiritual powers that have shaped the German bourgeoisie in the last few centuries are pietism, the Enlightenment, and Romanticism. Pietism was the last truly transformative religious movement on Lutheran soil. Out of a hopeless political reality, Luther led people into themselves and formed them into small, private circles. It was a religious individualism that strengthened the tendency to preoccupy oneself with psychological dissection and biographical contemplation. Every non-state, apolitical tendency had to find support and nourishment in pietistic Germany. The completely different individualism of the Enlightenment worked in the same direction. This individualism was not religious and sentimental, but based on reason — it was *rational*; it

---

3    Ghibellines were supporters of Frederick Barbarossa during his forays into Germanic Italy. Ghibellines, who tended to be agrarian, were pitted against the Guelphs, who were largely mercantile. [trans.]

was "political" only in its denial of the feudal system, but nevertheless incapable of building up its own permanent political system — it was merely capable of paving the way for the economic system of capitalism. Presented here was the sole individual, detached from all original orders and ties, a fictitious subject who only appeared responsible to himself. In contrast, Romanticism saw man again in his natural and historical ties. Romanticism has reopened our view for the night, the past and the ancestors, for myth and the people. The movement that leads from Herder to Görres, the Brothers Grimm, Eichendorff, Arnim and Savigny,[4] is the only spiritual movement still alive. It is also the only one with whom Nietzsche still wrestled.

It is no coincidence that Romanticism is still the least known movement in our history. The German bourgeoisie did not wholly accept it; they only appropriated what supported their worldview. Real Romanticism was opposed to the legend of Weimar Classicism, created by the conservative-liberal bourgeoisie. This legend is essentially formed from the elements of the Enlightenment fused with other — e.g., Romantic — elements. A great age of the German spirit, completely remote from the political sphere, was constructed by seeing Herder and Lessing, Schiller and Goethe, Humboldt and Hegel as one, and this construction was attributed to designating a "high point" in German history. It was precisely the most important thing of the epoch — the Ghibelline spirit — that lived on in it and was overlooked. Above all, it was misunderstood that this so-called "Classical" epoch has no independent roots. It is composed of Enlightenment-humaneness and the spirit and exertion of uncommon men. There is no such thing as a "spirit of the Age of Goethe." There is only one great solitary man who bears the name Goethe, and there is also an *artificial* synthesis that has been given the name "Classic." With the dissolution of the German bourgeoisie, this synthesis dissolves by itself, and the great individuals

---

4    Johann Gottfried Herder (d. 1803), Joseph Görres (d. 1848), Joseph Freiherr von Eichendorff (d. 1857), Achim von Arnim (d. 1831), Friedrich Carl von Savigny (d. 1861). [trans.]

become visible again: Lessing, the valiant fighter against Orthodoxy; Herder, the ancestor of Romanticism; and next to them, towering over them, the great solitary ones: Winckelmann,[5] Goethe, and Hölderlin. If we want to talk about Nietzsche's predecessors, then they deserve this name. This is what they share in common: an original, genuinely German, uncanny and incomprehensible relationship to Greece, which is not only of a formal, aesthetic kind, but also approaches Greek reality, Greek religiosity.

Calling National Socialism a worldview means that not only have the bourgeois parties been destroyed, but also their ideology. Only those filled with the most spiteful malevolence could presume that everything the past produced must now be denied. Rather, we have entered into a new relationship to the past; we have a clear view of the mighty thing in this formerly obscured bourgeois ideology; we have, in a word, found new possibilities to understand German essence. Here Nietzsche preceded us. Unlike him, however, we stand for Romanticism. But what was previously his most personal and solitary possession — the rejection of bourgeois ideology as a whole — is now the property of a generation.

I give an example of what so-called German Classicism has to offer. If the German bourgeoisie had not retired in the shadow of the Classical ideal they had invented, then it would have been possible that the basic concepts of Romanticism would have become political. But the political character of these concepts remained undeveloped. The German bourgeoisie proved incapable of conceiving an overall view. The political achievement of Bismarck corresponded to no idealistic achievement of the bourgeoisie. Treitschke is proof of this. All of Treitschke's personal temperament could not undo the Classicist legend of Weimar, which lies like a veiling fog over his theory of politics, nor could it help him gain a clear view into the world of power.

---

5    Johann Joachim Winckelmann (d. 1768) was a German Hellenist. [trans.]

Beyond the veiled ideology of the Classical period stands Nietzsche's stark sentence: *God is dead*. This is meant as a simple *historical* statement: belief in God has waned, God is no longer the power of our life. Nietzsche no longer "wrestles" with the Christian God — he doesn't even mourn his death. He is far from denying that Christians still exist — instead, he bows to them, finding a much higher type of person among them than, for example, among the artists of his time. In short, he is completely shorn of the resentment of the grappler who wants to break free. His knowledge of the death of the Christian God does not mean for him an "idea" that he would have to prove — he does not want the Christian God to be dead, but he sees in the end of *faith* in the Christian God the end of the Middle Ages in Europe.[6]

"I have no experience of any real religious troubles. It has completely escaped me to what extent I should be sinful…" Something like hatred only resonates when Nietzsche remembers his impressions as a young man, the pietistic-Romantic Christianity and Naumburg's yes-man hypocrisy [*Muckertum*]. "We, who were children in the swampy air of the fifties, are necessarily pessimists for the term *German*; we cannot be anything other than revolutionaries — we will not admit a state of affairs where the yes-man [*Mucker*] is on top."

Nietzsche criticizes Christianity, as he knew it, merely as an historical reality. He sees before him a tremendous phenomenon: the more the belief in God disappears, the more the idea of an inherently existing and self-established morality grows. That is the hallmark of the bourgeois state: *morality* instead of *religion*. The content of this morality supposedly coincides with the content of what might be called Christian moral teaching; thus, the transition occurs (at least

---

6   Baeumler is not trying to argue that Nietzsche was sympathetic to Christianity. He is saying that, for Nietzsche, spirituality — a *faith* — is preferable to the materialistic Nihilism flowing from the Enlightenment's rational-humanism. Liberalism (or *rationalism*) in all its forms — Nihilism, Christianity, globalism, communism, liberal-democracy, etc. — is poison for Nietzsche's vision of humanity. [trans.]

apparently) without a break. "You think you can get by with a moralism bereft of religious roots: with that, however, the path to Nihilism is opened."[7] "The Christian-moral God is not tenable: consequently 'atheism' — *as if there could be no other kind of gods.*"[8] "Basically only the moral God has been overcome."[9]

"Christianity has become something completely different from what its founder did and wanted." "That which is Christian in the ecclesiastical sense is anti-Christian from the start: nothing but things and people instead of symbols; nothing but history instead of eternal facts; nothing but formulas, rites, dogmas instead of a way of life. *Christian* is that complete indifference to dogmas, cult, priests, church, theology."[10] "It is an unparalleled abuse when such structures of decay and malformations as 'Christian Church,' 'Christian faith,' and 'Christian life' are identified with those holy names. What did Christ deny? *Everything that is called Christian today.*" Kierkegaard — the great Protestant of the North — could have said that too!

One will object: the way to the Church was necessary. Nietzsche replies: but then one also admitted that the way from the Gospel to the Church is the way into history with its orders and laws, i.e., the way into *politics*. For Nietzsche, the individual Christian is irrefutable. "Christianity is possible as the most private form of existence… A 'Christian state,' a 'Christian policy,' on the other hand, is shamelessness, a *lie*, like a Christian army leadership that ultimately treats the 'God of Hosts' as *chief of staff.*"[11] "Christianity is still possible at any moment…. Christianity is a *practice*, not a doctrine. It tells us how to *act*, not what to believe."[12] *Being a Christian* detaches from people,

---

7   *The Will to Power*, §19. [trans.]

8   *The Will to Power*, §151. [trans.]

9   *The Will to Power*, §55. [trans.]

10   *The Will to Power*, §159. [trans.]

11   *The Will to Power*, §211. [trans.]

12   *The Will to Power*, §212. [trans.]

state, cultural community, jurisdiction; it *rejects* teaching, knowledge, upbringing, acquisition, and commerce; one becomes apolitical, antinational, neither aggressive nor defensive. Anyone who does not want to be a soldier, who does not take care of the courts, who does not use the services of the police, who accepts every suffering in order to maintain inner peace — *that* would be a Christian. Nietzsche ridicules those who believe that Christianity has been overcome by natural science. "The Christian values are by no means overcome; 'Christ on the cross' is the most sublime symbol — still."[13]

The foundations of Christian morality: religious individualism, awareness of sin, humility, concern for the eternal salvation of the soul — these are completely *alien* to Nietzsche. He rebels against the idea of remorse: "I do not love this pusillanimity towards one's own actions; one should not abandon oneself under the onslaught of sudden shame and distress. *Extreme pride* is more appropriate. Lastly, what does it help! No deed is undone because of regret…"[14] What is meant here is not a slackening of responsibility, but an intensification. Nietzsche speaks from experience; he knows how much courage and pride it takes to stand in the face of fate. From his *amor fati*, Nietzsche speaks contemptuously of Christianity "with its perspective on salvation." As a Nordic man, he never understood why he should be "redeemed." The Mediterranean religion of salvation is *alien* and *distant* from his Nordic attitude. He can only understand man as a fighter against fate; a way of thinking that understands struggle and work only as punishment is inaccessible to him. "Our actual life is a false, fallen, sinful existence, a punishment…"[15] Suffering, struggle, work, and death are taken as objections to life. "Man as innocent, idle, immortal, happy — this conception of the 'highest desirability' is above all to be criticized." Nietzsche vehemently turns against the monk's

---

13   *The Will to Power*, §211. [trans.]

14   *The Will to Power*, §235. [trans.]

15   *The Will to Power*, §224. [trans.]

*vita contemplativa* [contemplative life], against Augustine's idea of the "Sabbath of Sabbaths." He praises Luther for having put an end to the *vita contemplativa*. The Nordic tone of struggle and work sounds strong and clear. The tone with which we pronounce these words today we first hear with Nietzsche.

We call Nietzsche the philosopher of *heroism*. This is only a half-understood truth if one does not also understand him as the philosopher of *activism*. He felt himself to be the historical antagonist of Plato. "Works" do not emerge from any empty show, the recognition of otherworldly values, but from practice, from repetitive action. To illustrate this, Nietzsche uses a famous antithesis. "First and foremost: *works*! That means *practice, practice, practice!* Faith will come later — rest assured of that!"[16] Against the Christian condemnation of the political sphere — the sphere of action in general — Nietzsche asserts his position, which surmounts the conflict between Catholicism and Protestantism ("*Faith* or *Works*?"): "Man must practice, not increasing feelings of value, but increasing *action*; one must first be able to act."[17] With this, he restores the purity of the sphere of action, the political sphere.

Nietzsche's "values" are not otherworldly and therefore cannot be turned into dogmas. They churn *in* and *through* us, and they only exist as long as we fight for them. When Nietzsche warns: *Stay true to the earth!*,[18] he reminds us of the idea rooted in our own strength, which does not wait for "realization" from some distant beyond. It is not enough to point out the "this-worldliness" of Nietzsche's values

---

16  *The Dawn*, §22. [trans.]

17  *The Will to Power*, §192. [trans.]

18  From "Zarathustra's Prologue" and "The Bestowing Virtue" (*Thus Spoke Zarathustra*), respectively: "I conjure you, my brethren, *remain true to the earth*, and believe not those who speak unto you of super-earthly hopes! Poisoners are they, whether they know it or not." "Remain *true to the earth*, my brethren, with the power of your virtue! Let your bestowing love and your knowledge be devoted to be the meaning of the earth!" [trans.]

if one does not at the same time refute the idea that values are "realized" through action. There is always something subaltern about the "realization" of given values, whether these are values of this world or the other world.

Through one's own strength, through the risk of action, values are created upon which all true order among people is built. Great historical forms of life can never be created through an individualistic morality — even if it is based on religious individualism. Nietzsche recognizes that traditional morality has paralyzed the spirit of action and made the establishment of historical orders impossible. According to this, there are only individual souls, there are no communities of anything more than temporary validity — no types, no "long, similar forms of activity." But the individual cannot assert himself as such — and so everything becomes an act. "Why everything becomes an *act.* — Modern man lacks the sure instinct (as a result of a *long, similar form of activity* in a type of man); the inability to achieve anything worthwhile is the consequence of this: — one individual alone cannot make up for the teaching his ancestors should have given him."[19] We are the furthest away from perfection in being, doing, and willing. "The extension of a will over long periods of time, the selection of the conditions and valuations that make it possible to have control over centuries in the future — that is precisely *anti-modern* in the highest sense."[20] Disorganizing principles give our age character: "abundant development of the intermediate forms, the decay of types."[21] National Socialism, in contrast, means the *recovery* of organizing principles and type-forming.

Nietzsche sees modern man's "acting" primarily as a consequence of the morality of "free will." This morality is related to a general overestimation of consciousness. "That the value of an action should depend

---

19   *The Will to Power*, §68. [trans.]

20   *The Will to Power*, §65. [trans.]

21   *The Will to Power*, §74. [trans.]

on what preceded it in consciousness — how wrong is that!"[22] "Every perfect action is precisely unconscious and unintentional; consciousness expresses an imperfect and often pathological personal state.... Any degree of consciousness makes perfection *impossible*.... A form of *acting*."[23] "Just as the soldier drills, so should a man learn to act in life. In fact, such unconsciousness belongs to every kind of perfection: even the mathematician calculates unconsciously...."[24] Unconsciousness, practice, perfection. "We must seek the perfect life where it is least conscious...."[25] This is different from the liberal doctrine of "personality," which has a) principles and b) an individuality that outshines its principles. Nietzsche does not begin with principles, but rather with values that serve a specific race, although this "conservation" should not be understood too narrowly: it is about the preservation of the race *with all its values*. "In all valuations there is a definite purpose: the preservation of an individual, a community, a race, a state, a church, a faith, a culture."[26] There is nothing that is valuable in itself without reference to an existence. Values express conditions of existence. Therefore, false values cannot be eradicated by reason: it is existence against existence.

Nietzsche's Nordic, martial values stand against the Mediterranean, priestly ones. His criticism of religion is a criticism of the priest,[27] and it comes from the standpoint of the warrior, in that Nietzsche proves that the origin of religion also lies in the realm of power. This is where the fatal contradiction of morality based on the Christian religion comes from. "In order for moral values to prevail, immoral forces and passions must help them. The emergence of moral values is the

---

22  *The Will to Power*, §291. [trans.]

23  *The Will to Power*, §289. [trans.]

24  *The Will to Power*, §430. [trans.]

25  *The Will to Power*, §439. [trans.]

26  *The Will to Power*, §259. [trans.]

27  See, too, *Ecce Homo* ("Why I Am A Fate"): "I am not a man, I am dynamite.... Religions are matters for the mob." [trans.]

work of immoral passions and considerations."²⁸ Morality is therefore
the work of immorality. "How to Bring Virtue to Rule: This treatise is
about the great politics of virtue." It is intended to be taught for the first
time: "that one can only achieve the rule of virtue through the same
means with which one achieves rule in general, in any case not by
virtue itself."²⁹ — "One must be very immoral in order to *create morality* through deeds."³⁰ Nietzsche replaces bourgeois moral philosophy
with the philosophy of the *will to power*, i.e., the philosophy of *politics*.
If he becomes a eulogist of the "unconscious," then this unconscious
cannot be understood in the sense of depth psychology.³¹ It is not a
question of the individual's instinctual unconsciousness; rather, "unconscious" means something like "perfect" or "skilled." Furthermore,
the unconscious means life in general, the organism, the "great reason"
of the body.

Consciousness is just a tool, a detail in the whole of life. Nietzsche
contrasts the aristocracy of Nature with the philosophy of consciousness. For thousands of years, however, a morality that is hostile to life
has been working against the aristocracy of the strong and healthy. Like
National Socialism, Nietzsche sees the state and society as the "grand
mandatary of life," which has to answer for every failed life before life
itself. "The species needs the downfall of the botched, the weak, the
degenerate: but it is precisely to them that Christianity is directed as
a preservative force..."³² Here we come across the fundamental contradiction: one can assume a natural view of life, or one can imagine
the equality of individual souls before God. The democratic ideal of
equality ultimately rests on the latter assumption; the former contains

---

28  *The Will to Power*, §266. [trans.]

29  *The Will to Power*, §304. This section is called "How to Bring Virtue to Rule."
    [trans.]

30  *The Will to Power*, §397. [trans.]

31  Depth psychology [*Tiefenpsychologie*] is the study of the unconscious and its
    relationship to the conscious. [trans.]

32  *The Will to Power*, §246. [trans.]

the foundations of a new policy. There is unheard of audacity in basing the state on race. A new order must result from this. It is the order that Nietzsche wanted to restore over and against the existing one.

Given the supremacy of the species, where does this leave the individual? He is coming back — as an individual in a community. The herd instinct is something fundamentally different from the instinct of an "aristocratic society." Strong, natural men are returning — men who do not let their basic instincts atrophy in favor of a useful mediocrity, men who discipline their passions instead of weakening or destroying them. This, too, should not be understood from the perspective of the individual. The passions have to be "tyrannized" for a long time. Only a community, a race, a people can do that.

The justification of passion, of the body, of Nature is a justification of reality in general. With the addition of a creative subject, a perpetrator, to reality, Nietzsche sees the destruction of the "innocence of becoming." The creative task is to restore the two spheres of reality, Nature and History. These same spheres are being restored by National Socialism. The artificiality of absolute opposites according to the scheme of *good* and *evil* are replaced by the natural hierarchy of *better* and *worse*. And in the light of this natural hierarchy, history takes on a new meaning.

The manly age, the age of workers and soldiers, predicted by Nietzsche, is dawning. Every culture defines the relationship between men and women in its own way. The place that man will occupy in the coming age has become visible, but that of woman has not yet. The woman will also find her place in this new interrelation. Read what Nietzsche said about the Greek woman.

The realistic, Nordic-manly [*nordisch-männlich*] attitude is expressed above all in the distrust of "happiness," of beatitude, of "contentment in contemplative states," whether one looks for it in the eyes of a loved one ("adoration") or in striking works of art. Man does not seek pleasure or avoid pain, Nietzsche teaches, but rather he seeks more power. Out of his will to power, he looks for resistance, because the will to power is the *will to overcome fate*. "The degree of resistance that must be constantly overcome in order to remain on top is the measure of freedom, be it for individuals or for societies: namely, freedom is seen as positive power, as the *will to power*."[33] The highest type grows where the highest resistance must constantly be overcome. "One must need to be strong, otherwise one will never become strong."[34]

If there is a German maxim, it is this: *One must need to be strong, otherwise one will never become strong*. We Germans know what it means to assert ourselves in the face of resistance. We understand the "will to power" — albeit in a completely *different* way than our opponents imagine. Nietzsche also said the most profound thing about this: "We Germans want something from ourselves that no one has yet wanted from us — *we want something more!*"[35]

When we see the German youth marching today under the Swastika, we recall Nietzsche's *Untimely Meditations*, in which this youth was addressed for the first time.[36] It is our greatest hope that the state is open to these young people today. And when we call out to this youth *Heil Hitler!* — we also greet Friedrich Nietzsche.

---

33   *The Will to Power*, §770. [trans.]

34   *Twilight of the Idols*, §38. [trans.]

35   *The Will to Power*, §108. [trans.]

36   For example, Part II, §9: "Whether our lives and culture are threatened by these dissolute, toothless and tasteless greybeards or by ... so-called 'men,' let us in the face of both hold on with our teeth to the rights of our youth and never weary in our youth of defending the future against these iconoclasts who would wreck it. In this struggle, however, we shall have to discover a particularly unpleasant fact: *that the excesses of the historical sense from which the present day suffers are deliberately furthered, encouraged, and — employed.*" Excerpted from *Untimely Meditations* (Cambridge University, 1983), translated by J. Hollingdale. [trans.]

# Europe's New Order as Historical-Philosophical Problem

## 1.

THE SO VERY WISE and industrious men who in 1919 dictated "peace" to the stunned and exhausted peoples of Versailles had information from all over the world, their desks covered with extremely "exact" numbers; what could have possibly eluded their curiosity? Who thought more realistically than these financiers, economists, and diplomats? What *refined* calculations, what an amassing of ingenious ruses, what an abundance of "decisive" meetings and conferences! And yet — who suspected what was actually going on in those weeks of 1919? Who could have dreamed this pretentious game of *values*, this highly rationalized stock-exchange business, was in reality the death-dance of a millennium? The sober calculators who thought they had the world in their grasp would have ironically fended it off if they had been declared ghosts. Though, what is a ghost but a being that does not move in accordance with the law, but instead moves by some mysterious unreality? Don't they seem possessed by a demonic power forcing them to do the opposite of what they "actually" want, these Versailles peacemakers? Is there a single representative of real power among them who could be seen as the executor of his own will and destiny? All the power of earth was in their hands — yet they could do nothing; they determined and arranged without end — and — not order, but *chaos* emerged. It is the false worshipers of power who must finally realize they are being fooled by their idol. Those who seemed so powerful — a moment later they lost the ground under their feet, they float into nothing, they have become ghosts.

The fiendish transformation of violence into nonviolence, of apparent strength into utter weakness, has never before been seen; never have there been more wretched men on earth than the victors of Versailles; never before has violence been so radically led to absurdity. In addition to the countless practical consequences of the famous peace conference, the symbolic significance of this event must not be forgotten.

If today we no longer care to know the spirituality once triumphant in the West, then one of the most important reasons for our turning away lies in the complete failure of Western ideology before the appearance and concept of *power*. We can say without hyperbole: if the lie had not been a basic element of the Western spirit, then such a monstrous lie, because it was organized and analyzed down to the last detail (like the "peace work" of Versailles), could never have happened. One has to have learned something like that; it cannot be improvised. Only men raised from childhood to disguise realities and to speak a language of unreality could manage to give the most brutal instrument that ever existed, the *Versailles Peace Instrument*, a conceptual form that fundamentally ignores the facts and idea of power. Every carving away and reassigment of territory, every establishment of new power structures, was justified with phrases of *humanity* and *justice* that no one took seriously. The same men who wielded violence in every form with true virtuosity expressed themselves publicly and "responsibly" as if power in itself were evil. There is nothing more corrupting than the constant divergence of language and action. *Versailles was no accident*; only one system could commit this crime. The system which produced the *lie of all lies* believed that at the end of the First World

War it was at the height of its power; in the Second World War it fights its death throes.

The proposition that power in itself is *evil* — which comes from a good-hearted German moralist and was adopted by Jacob Burckhardt — was invented to defend humanity. In effect, however, this idea reveals itself as one of the most *inhumane* errors of a misled Western civilization. It conceals essential differences that must be made if any human order is to exist. If all power is evil, then no distinction can be made between power and "power" — that is, between real and apparent power. But *every* true political order is based on this distinction. An order can only be called *true* if it gives form and endurance to a condition established in the real context of things. This connection is not easy to see. It is hidden in life's depths and by no means always coincides with existing parameters. Of course, it is more difficult to see than the sum of the existing facts. In committees and at conferences, however, it is the *facts* that usually speak; deeper connections are condemned to silence. War reveals a reality that destroys appearances and exposes truth. Peoples measure each other in war, and in this struggle their true relationship is laid bare — independent of *peace conferences.*

Power is neither good nor bad because power does not exist. Power is a constituent of life; "evil" can be called *power based on false, life-contradicting assumptions.* But it is more correct to call it *mendacious* and *false* rather than *evil.* If one asserts that *every* state of power contains evil and contradiction, then this is nothing short of a libel on life. Rather, any state of power that corresponds to a real state of life is *good.* Politics is the art of harmonizing exisiting states of power with that which is *alive in the depths.* This has to happen again and again; life constantly changes and with it, power. What persists amidst this change are the natural-historical *communities,* the *peoples* — and the power we are talking about here is not a subjective drive for power, but that objective essential element in the existence of peoples, without which stability and peace always remain a mere dream.

## 2.

The idea of peace is a fundamental concept of Western civilization. It would be *incomprehensible* that the thousand-year rule of a thought so useful, so captivating to man could lead to an age of world wars, unless the structure of this concept in its Western form was not in some way flawed. If we, who have been led to the brink of ruin and death by error, examine the Western idea of peace with an unbiased mind, prompted by the danger around us, the following results:

There is no doubt that the Western idea of peace means *absolute* peace. The ideal state of affairs is one without disputes, a world peace without struggle, an eternal balance between peoples without conflict. Peace in this sense is beyond discussion. Anyone who has a different concept of peace is an agitator from the start. But what must become of a civilization if its central concept, which has such worth, is *wrong*? The age of world wars gave us the answer. It is as if the second of these wars had been necessary to preclude any interpretation of the first as a mere exception. The First World War was not an accident, it was not a mistake: it was the revelation of the abysmal *contradiction* we have so long accepted as the Western spirit.

Not only the individual failed in this terrible crisis — a *system of thinking* has also reached its utmost limit. The idea of absolute ("eternal") peace turned out not only to be incapable of properly shaping this world, but also defiled those who believed it — or pretended to believe it. Reality cannot be maintained with incorrect ideas.

Thoughts meant to become *political* must have an objective relationship to reality. Even the most beautiful dream will have a destructive effect if it does not meet the conditions of its realization. *Peace* only has political value if it is related to the nature and character of the subjects for whom it is supposed to exist: the people. It was the West's fate to chase after an *inhuman* idea of peace for centuries.

*Inhuman* is not only that which is *beneath* the sphere of human values and order, but also that which is *impossible for humans to realize* — that is, the *superhuman*. Certainly, one must never be satisfied with what is positively given in the coincidental interplay of things. Positivism — unassuming as it is — corresponds to a certain tendency to laziness, for which man repeatedly falls. It is *ideas* that wrest people from the spell of factualities and direct their will towards distant goals. We must never lose this most practical sense of the *idea*. It would be a fatal error, however, to think it enough to have sublime and splendid ideas, and the rest can be left to God. One who puts an idea into action also takes responsibility for what develops under the rule of this idea. One must not imagine this responsibility can be evaded by appealing to the *goodness* and *beauty* of an idea, by looking to the inadequacy of the individual for the fact that only misfortune arises under its rule. We are never exempt from examining ideas for their suitability to people and the powers given to them; and even a tradition that is yet revered today must not prevent us from making this criticism.

The dream of absolute peace is "inhuman" because it interposes itself through all human reality. The *superhuman*, which has no responsible relation to man, has just as fatal an effect as the *subhuman* when it replaces the *human*.

Peace has two sides, as it were: on the one hand it is harmony, on the other it is power. A harmony that would not be power at the same time is not a political condition. When peace is glorified, the power underlying this condition is deliberately overlooked. The beauty and advantages of a struggle-free order are extolled without asking about the *means* by which it can be established. But the means could *only* be an absolute power. Only if it were possible to *eliminate all particularities* could a universal peace be established. But every condition of power is tied to the nature of the people who realize it and for whom it exists. An absolute condition of power *presupposes the disappearance of all natural and historical differentiations between people*, i.e., the elimination of national individualities. We are not against the dream of eternal peace because we are against peace, but because it is at the same time a dream of absolute power. Absolute peace seems a glorious, superhuman idea; absolute power is an *inhuman* idea. A power that has lost all particularity and individuality has lost all human-historical power to *be* power. *To have power* belongs solely to the concept of the human being and the community in which he can live, develop, and perfect himself.

The idea of eternal peace is abstract and universal; conditions of power are always concrete and particular. A power cannot exist without a subject, a bearer of power, also existing. But these subjects and carriers cannot be *general* any more than man can be a *general* subject. The thought of a general peace is therefore, from a human and historical point of view, an *un-thought*, because it presupposes an impossible general subject. Practically speaking, it means the ideological attempt to abolish peoples as independent political entities by establishing an absolute power. England attempted this when it rose to become the world's police force in the 19th century. The history of the "West" ends with the failure of this gigantic enterprise.

Spiritually, the attempt to realize "eternal" peace with the help of an absolute power leads to fundamental political hypocrisy. Every real power has a certain depth of being lost when the bearer of power is universalized in an inhuman and fantastic way. All being wants to assert itself. It is a law of life that the depth of being demanding self-assertion can never be given up in favor of any universality. Denial of the will to assert oneself may lead to interesting and historically effective phenomena in the religious sphere — in the political sphere, however, it is what theologians call the "fall into sin."

The essence of power has always been seen in self-assertion. What one could no longer see in the last few centuries, blinded by false conceptions of man, was that the exercise and use of power are inseparable from man. Likewise, an abuse of power must never lead to a denial of power in the *non-concept* of an absolute power. Every abuse of power contains the demand to put true power in place of the wrong one and to think about the terms of real power conditions and relations — a reflection that can be meaningful and successful only within the framework of an impartial self-image of the human being. Power in itself is neither good nor bad; it is *human* and must be handled according to the laws of life.

Never has a greater crime been committed against life than the so-called Treaty of Versailles. At that time, the right of peoples to self-determination was not only upheld, it was even made a principle. At the same time, however, this right was violated in the most refined and brutal way by the "idea" of absolute peace, i.e., absolute power. *To proclaim the idea of perpetual peace and simultaneously cling to the self-determination of peoples is a grave contradiction.* In political practice the contradiction becomes a lie. Versailles is, in fact, something like a high point in Western history; there are consequences with the lie. The accursed name under which the lie of all lies went into the world was that of the *Société des Nations* [League of Nations].

It is a glory of the German spirit that this term, which was supposed to designate the most hideous hubris of absolute power, can only be conveyed in the German language by the simple and beautiful word *Völkerbund*. At the end of every honestly fought dispute there must be a "covenant" of the peoples who have struggled with one another. This is what the righteousness of life demands. Drawing false conclusions from a temporary superiority is careless and cultivates revenge; a bad peace is political stupidity. But it is a crime against humanity when brutal violence poses as the embodiment of eternal peace and crowns a long, bloody struggle with the establishment of a *society of nations*.[1] The Versailles Peace Conference has not only been imposed on the eternal will to live of many nations, it has also treated the honor and the intellect of these peoples with contempt. For reason tells us there is justice in life; but there can only be deceitful manipulation

---

1    Baeumler occasionally uses "society of nations" [*Gesellschaft der Nationen*] instead of "League of Nations" [*Völkerbund*] to apparently highlight the spiritually empty *society* [*Gesellschaft*] character of the League, as opposed to a genuine, spiritually rich *community* [*Gemeinschaft*] character that might exist in a more just world. [trans.]

behind it if it is claimed that the aim of the struggle was a glorious, everlasting order — an order under the Bank of England's dictatorship and Britain's police supervision. The League of Nations' "eternal peace" revealed both the inadequacy of the politicians who hatched it and a shifting of Western thought, which allowed a *façade* of justice to be laid before the most undignified system of violence — the *plutocratic* one. The assembly hall in Geneva, which was only the most despised and unsightly antechamber of the London rooms in which world politics were decided by a spiritually and politically degenerate ruling class, will always remain the symbol of an abuse of power with which few others in all of world history can compete. If the powers that invented the *society of nations* impose the catchword *democracy* on the free peoples of Europe again today, it is a sign of intellectual torpor; but it is also a stroke of fate, for the inevitable downfall of those powers will also put an end to the shameful term *democracy*, which the masses sacrificed to the Moloch of absolute power.

Against the will of its authors, the lie of Versailles, by virtue of the dialectic of history, brought about a great purification of a dank atmosphere. The peoples themselves rose up and answered the politicians. Through the foolish violation of their right to live, the fiery will of nations had been fanned into fanaticism. Immediately following the peace *diktat*, and as a result of it, the movement reached its consummation: *nationalism* had awakened. The classic epoch of European nationalism begins in 1914; the 19th century is its archaic preliminary stage. Versailles, with its violation of the rights of the peoples, has culminated in a development that goes back to Western history's nascence.

### 3.

Western history began not with the self-awareness of individual peoples, but the idea of a general cultural mission. "Western" is not the epitome of emerging nations, but a religious task that goes beyond all nations. Executing this task creates an inner cultural unity around which, from some racial core, the peoples determining Europe's history coalesce. This gives rise to the strange double-nature of this story: the emergence of *particular* national units occurs within the framework of a *universal* cultural idea. National characters force their way into the light; all their expressions, however, are absorbed by a spiritual universalism which, while permitting the formation of varied *impulses*, is unable to aid in the decisive development of a healthy, clear national *consciousness*. Religious universalism, which is only one side of religious individualism, must leave folkish [*völkisch*] communities to develop and interpret their being on their own. The result is that political history and intellectual development go their separate ways: intellectual history, which is essentially determined by religion, follows its course; political history, which mainly consists in the formation of nations into autonomous social bodies, follows its course. Separate developments of individual peoples and ideologies work against each other because they arise from separate impulses. This divergence is not accidental. It is *impossible* for ideology to do justice to the innermost concern of the peoples to understand themselves as historical units. And, it is an *existential* question for individual peoples to develop a unified national consciousness. This process must take place in the underworld, as it were, since religious ideology is not politically determinate. General concepts of love and peace accompany it, which has certain educational effects, but these must leave political formation and the development of national languages to immanent forces. The European peoples grow amidst the resulting tensions. *National* consolidation proceeds relentlessly; the *universal* ideology asserts itself with the greatest tenacity. National units use religion as a means of fusing; it intervenes deeply in popular education and connects with popular life. However, none of this can prevent the persistent contradiction between politics and spirit.

Religious wars, the characteristic phenomenon of European history, arise from the amalgamation of national and religious tendencies.

Modern Europe was finally formed when these struggles reached their peak in the 16th and 17th centuries. Western religiosity's political impotence leads to spiritually immature national powers using religious fervor to develop unnatural political pathos. The artificial overstraining of nationalism in Europe can be traced back to this process. Accounting this strain to inherent national dispositions is an historical error. Rather, it is an historically unique phenomenon; since it has arisen from certain conditions, it can also change with them.

What has been prevented by this process is more obscure than the positive, if disastrous, influence universalism has exerted on national development. By transferring its universalism to individual national particularities, the idea of universal religion can lead to intemperate exaggerations and inflamed national passions. It can never, however, create the justice inherent in the history of the peoples themselves because it cannot create the prerequisite for this: the idea of focused human-historical communities and their right *not* to allow universalism to arise at all. There can be no doubt universalism encouraged political enthusiasm and, in the age of nationalism, led to more than a little hypocrisy. No one can say what would have happened *spiritually* if the peoples had been left to their own devices. Development would have been slower in many respects, but no one can claim that it would have been impossible for the peoples to develop an appropriate conception of national existence and international relations.

Confronting us is a process that can only be explained by a lack of political focus in individual nations. In the end, Western civilization had a brilliant ideological façade; spiritually unguided and unsupervised, behind a venerable, glistening face in the dark, national wills wrestled with each other. Unguided by a political idea, the West headed for the abyss. The latest events of this civilization are the most terrible wars in world history. The two world wars are deliberately fought as *religious* wars by the "democracies" using old memories. Whether it is the "Central Powers" or the "totalitarian states" — world democracy, which has constituted itself as *absolute power*, declares *war* on the "others" *in the name of eternal justice* and *peace*.

If life could be deduced,[2] then under universalism's rule, the understanding between national will-subjects [*Willenssubjekten*] would occur in the manner of a syllogism. The unifying universal does not need to be laboriously sought; it is given and meets everyone with the utmost urbanity as an unconditional moral demand. A more favorable condition for the formation of a political power superior to all particular tendencies is apparently inconceivable. And yet the actual historical process teaches us that precisely the opposite is the case. Nations are not minor premises in a logical conclusion, but *unfathomable realities* arising from their own depths of being; they did not *spring* from the idea[3] and therefore do not *conform* to the idea. National existence cannot be guided by something *external*; this being is not fulfilled in submission to a form coming from above, but in the search for one's *own* form. It is only through their history, and not through the realization of a given universal, that the peoples come to themselves. Their basic tendency is not of *classification*, but of *self-assertion*, by which all submission to the universal is sharply rejected. At the beginning of all politics is the *healthy egoism* of the peoples. Frederick the Great's definition from his 1752 political testament holds: "Politics is the art of always acting in accordance with one's own interests by all suitable means."

Universalism's claim to dominance can thus lead to the opposite of its intent. The universal does not triumph over the particular, but the particular gladly takes note of the pathos and the unconditionality of the universal and uses them for its own purposes. Only from this dialectic can the peculiarly intricate structure of the European nations' self-consciousness be explained.

---

2   That is, as a purely mechanical process, without the irrationality inherent in man. [trans.]

3   That is, the idea of *universalism*. [trans.]

The universalistic ideals of one humanity and one peace have had the historical task of making nascent nations emphatically aware of their own individuality, precisely through their inner *contradiction* to these objectives. Such intensification of individuality may have fruitful consequences in the field of culture — politically, however, it must have *catastrophic* consequences. Every natural force carries within itself the striving for assertion and development; an intensification of these natural tendencies is not desired. In the sphere of spirit, *individualization* taken to extremes can perhaps spark the sublime; in the sphere of politics, it leads to impotence or to an all-exclusive arrogance (France and England offer great European examples). It is politically destructive in both cases. The greatest value in political action is *measure*, which alone guarantees the endurance to which all actions serving self-assertion are directed. Power always seeks to sustain itself. No power gives up on itself — power never concedes voluntarily. Endurance is part of the essence of every state of power. In political terms, "measure" does not mean a reflection of eternal harmonies, but something very simple and realistic: a law of life, the prerequisite for permanent self-assertion. All excess consumes itself; *being* fits in with this order and is therefore eternal.

Because they obscure this law of life, universalism's ideals are necessarily destructive. Such generality obscures the view; the natural striving of tangible powers is ignored or unrecognized. Political thinking loses the ground under its feet through universalism: it becomes bottomless, excessive, fanatical — it deals in fictions, not realities. Alienation from measured power-thinking [*Machtdenken*] is the root of all political disaster.

Self-realization is the fundamental tendency of all power. The problem of power, and the political problem in general, begins with a practical interpretation of what preserves it in individual cases. Stagnation is inimical to life, for life is always a back and forth, an up or down, a more or less; it can only go forwards or backwards, but not stop. "Stagnation means regression." Measure is not inherent to power;

it must be brought to it. Power bears a restlessness which is incessantly driving beyond itself. This is the *pleonexia* [greed] of power of which Aristotle spoke. In reality, the tendency towards preservation is almost always interpreted as meaning that only an expansion of power can guarantee its preservation. The problem of politics is the *limitation* of power, i.e., the scaling down of the natural tendency towards preservation in the form of wanting more in the measure of being.

Power cannot be left to itself. Just as the rich are never rich enough for themselves, the powerful are never powerful enough for themselves. The fate of the Western spirit consisted in the fact that it viewed *pleonexia* as a curse and did not recognize that it concealed the healthy will for self-preservation. The second error consisted in trying to remove the wrongly judged evil by wrong means. Logically the particular is opposed to the universal, but, politically, the striving of particular powers cannot be tamed by the universal — because a power can only ever be tamed by another power or by something related to the power, but not by something that is on a completely different level. The political impotence of all universal ideas has been sufficiently proven.

But where should we look for that which lies on the same plane of being as power and yet has the ability to tame power? There is no such thing as a universal power, so it cannot be that. As long as there is only power against power, war is declared permanently; a principle of international order limiting war would be inconceivable.

## 4.

One of the few things democracy understands is the exploitation of intellectual laziness in favor of anti-German propaganda. It is so easy to declare to the world that National Socialism rejects peace *because it recognizes the law of struggle*; that it is an opponent of understanding *because it finds the idea of a world order upheld by a global police force ridiculous*. Nobody has it easier than someone who appeals to old ways of thinking. It is National Socialism's weakness that it requires people to think. People, whom we do not by chance call *creatures of habit*, prefer to do anything rather than think — because thinking means breaking free from habits.

The sweet habit of viewing every tangible peace as a mere preparation for eternal peace, of thinking of an even higher state of power by which it is kept in check, the delusion that a power could be made to set limits for itself through ideologies — National Socialism left all of this behind forever. Our worldview demands from everyone the abandonment of all prejudices and an understanding able to recognize the world as it is. When we say *race*, we think not only of the diversity of racial types that experience demonstrates, but, above all, of a general law of life: the law that like is produced only by like, and that living forces are constant.

The discovery of race recalls a state of affairs akin to medieval alchemy. As long as one did not know the *constancy of forces*, it was possible to indulge in fantastic ideas about the development and transformation of natural forces, ideas that resembled those of the goldmakers. One day, it was thought, gold production *must* be obtained; one day, so philosophers believed — and, at least, the politicians pretended to believe — eternal peace *must* be achieved. Knowledge of race as the *enduring* and *creative* force in every people puts modern *science* in the place of medieval *dreams*. This knowledge removes old errors, giving new and fruitful impulses to thinking. Human history no longer appears as an accumulation of error and violence; the governing law is now discernible. In recognizing this law of human forces, our eyes open to a realistic view of historical reality in general. At the same time as the conditions of race, the conditions of space[4] come into our field of vision. Where previously mysterious entities were drifting about, phenomena are now arranged into clearly comprehensible units, the connection of which presents us with new tasks.

---

4    Baeumler did not use the term *Lebensraum*, but *Raum*. The context here and in later paragraphs, however, suggests his "space" means "living space," or "living area." [trans.]

History, which is determined by the realities of race and space, is dynamic. Wherever people relate to one another, we see forces wrestling with one another. History is not the evolution of some unitary substance, but a living *opposition* and *coexistence* of substantial forces. Forces build the structures of power whose creation, expansion, decay, or self-assertion the historian tracks. A philosophy of history fertilized by the idea of race has recognized how much confusion has been caused by not keeping the categories of force and power separate and repeatedly transferring the determinations of one reality to the other. Thus the law of power to assert oneself through expansion has always been equated with the striving of a force for activity. This made the correct assessment of both realities impossible. A dignity was ascribed to the derived structure of power which it does not have. Natural creative *forces*, on the other hand and in hindsight, have been burdened with everything *power* has ever caused. Destruction wrought by this misunderstanding reaches to the very depths of being. Power was increased by all that belonged to the *force* and then cursed; the sphere of innocence, in which living forces freely move, was dragged into the darkness of this curse and fell into contempt. With this, the conditions necessary for a human, appropriate treatment of political problems were destroyed.

Power has its own law. Precisely because it is *not* a force, but a reality with its own structure, it exhibits that repeatedly criticized property, *pleonexia*. A state of power can exist independent from the forces that produced it for a long time, and it can increase itself out of itself. In this case, power breaks away from living forces, becomes abstract and proliferates. Once a dominance develops recognized and functional forms, these forms continue to exist, as it were, by virtue of their own authority — often against all living forces that stir in the community. *That* is the mode of power which has given, in and for itself, this human and necessary structure to the hatred of the times.

## 5.

The point is not to suppress power but to give it a *human* form. Is it so dangerous that every power likes to voluntarily expand but never voluntarily restrict itself? This would only be disastrous *if there were nothing to limit expansion.* As long as one has to wait until another power arises in order to limit the expanding power, we cannot escape a state of war. It is precisely the hallmark of the modern world, which pays homage to the idea of peace, that it does not know how to oppose *pleonexia.* Under the guise of humanitarian phrases hides the most *unrestrained veneration of violence* world history has ever seen: "struggle" and "war" are maligned, the soldier is seen as a holdover from backward times, the farmer is despised. Only commerce and money are sacred to democratic-bourgeois society. *Stock exchange* and *civilization* are inseparable ideas here, the spell of *gold* dominates the mind. Economy is destiny. An obvious, unspeakable secret is key to all manifestations of the democratic system: *power must nowhere be seen.* The principle of leadership is hidden behind parliamentarism, rule is only permitted in the most dishonest, cruel, and most pathetic of all forms — as *rule of money.* Power takes the form of *siphoning off* [*Aussaugung*]. There are only the rich who have everything and the poor who have nothing. Democratic "freedom" consists in perpetuating belief in the *have-nots* that they can one day rise to the ranks of the *haves* by means of free acquisition. Everyone can do what he likes, this ideology proclaims — advancement or starvation is up to you. The truth is, a small stratum of immeasurably wealthy men hold rulership in their merciless hands, which is *not to be discussed in public.* Those who have money participate in rule, those who do not belong to the millions of slaves of the plutocratic system.

Since the principle of economic "freedom" prevails (everyone can buy and sell as much as they "want"), the system of *naked violence* is at the same time the system of *freedom.* This cunning hypocrisy is only possible because dominion has taken the form of economic exploitation and become invisible. There is no real representation — parliaments are only there to *prevent* any representation. Modern democracy is in every way a system of absolute duplicity — it is *compulsion* with a veneer of "freedom."

The same principle of *siphoning off* also applies to foreign policy, which is essentially colonial policy. The colonies are ruthlessly exploited: they have raw materials and soldiers to deliver. What becomes of the peoples inhabiting the conquered territories of distant realms is inconsequential. Equally irrelevant is whether or not the raw materials are responsibly extracted and whether the products obtained satisfy *needs* existing elsewhere on earth. The only decisive factor is *profit*. Plutocratic society is insatiable in its hunger for gold: peoples die, lands are made desolate — but profits rise. The only thing that matters is the increase in wealth, and the security and luxury wealth guarantees.

A democratic state consists of a small number of excessively wealthy people who consider it their only political responsibility to make others work for them. It makes no difference whether the others are compatriots [*Volksgenossen*], colonial slaves, or allies. The web of treaties [*Garantieverträge*] Great Britain often weaved around nations is a distinctive expression of plutocracy's parasitic thinking. In accordance with capital's essence, its power seeks to peak more and more: it grows *indefinitely*. A treaty only makes sense if real forces back it. Great Britain's treaties, offered to every accessible state, were disconnected from all reality; beneficial to the British for a moment, they all but destroyed the nations under treaty. Democratic politicians did not care for a moment which living forces were drawn into the afflicted state's downfall, whether valuable folkdom [*Volkstum*] was destroyed in the process. The coldest *will to rule* made its calculation in the icy space of empty power.

An Englishman can unselfconsciously say: *We don't have a square meter of land outside of our own borders; what we have is just the friendship of those who own the land.* He only forgets a little something: "friendship" means only *control over the money*, i.e., over the work of those to whom the land was left for processing. One does not speak of the power of money. It is true that trade follows the flag, but not that friendship as a political phenomenon presupposes the gentle *coercion of capital*, without which it would probably be subject to excessive fluctuations.

Every power is concurrently negative and positive: it can only build up by rejecting or fighting what stands in its way. The power of capital differs from every other form of power in that, although it achieves dazzling instant successes, it never has an edifying effect. Its main means is credit, which happens to be aid issued out of pure "pragmatism" and sheer "understanding." In fact, it is the noose that slips around the neck of the "economically weaker." All you have to do is gently tighten — the use of force is *prohibited* — and the victim writhes on the ground. A great democratic power is characterized by the fact that it can grant loans. As long as people are foolish enough to believe in money, as long as they can be ruled by credit withdrawals — this is the formula for Jewish-democratic world domination. If everything is money and money is everything, the "world" can never be more than the playground of corporations and stockmarket speculators. Financial empires have no human interest in a nation or its people. Capital only ever wants to increase itself; it ruthlessly runs over all factual connections along the way. Protection of *vital forces*, be it the forces of a nation or of the soil, respect for Nature, consideration of other wills to live — these are ridiculous concepts to money interests. Pure financial thinking achieves success after success and draws all destructive people into its circle — only to one day encounter the realities it denies. The most abstract form of power we know, whose striving for *more* apparently nothing can stop, ultimately fails because of the reality of the vital forces it has denied.

Rightly speaking, one cannot talk of democratic "states" at all. A state only exists when a self-determined political order arises from a living people. There are no democratic *states*, there is only a democratic *society* that, with the help of its banks, oversees so-called states.

This society is *one*; it has representatives all over the world — in Europe as well as in Africa, America and Australia. Historically, it succeeded the supranational feudal ruling class of earlier times. The supranational chivalrous society was the Middle Ages' universalism; the pseudo-universalism of modern times, which is no longer believed, corresponds to the plutocratic upper class, which, until recently, either owned or controlled the production of raw materials and trade all over the world. London is still the center of this wealthy ruling class today. Over time, a second center formed in America which, not so long ago, London deigned to look upon with barely veiled contempt. The ideal of the *rich man* is the same here and there. The stratum of *rich men* sets the tone; how they think, how they live, how they dress — this is absolutely decisive for anyone who wants to matter on this earth. A *rich man* should not be imagined as a millionaire in the European way. Poor people are not spoken of here. One only knows what *richness* is where plutocracy originated. People who have no idea what it means to exploit Egypt and India cannot imagine the wealth of an English lord. Even less can they guess what magical effect emanates from this wealth. The world has not been conquered in the last few centuries by liberal "ideas" or by the English way of life (all this only followed) — no, *it was conquered by the rich*. Freemasonry is one, but by no means the only, form through which the rich influenced the "states." Only when the idol of money no longer enchants the world will the rule of that small stratum be over, which in every so-called capital city lets its representatives, their banknotes, and a few other things circulate. The end of plutocracy is the birth of *national states*. After the disempowerment of the international moneyed class, everywhere men can take power for whom "peace" means something other than a moralistic phrase used to camouflage *business*. These men are the leaders of their peoples. They are liable with their lives to ensure peace is maintained, the honor and security of the nation. For these leaders, airplanes are not ready and waiting to whisk them away to a secure location.[5] Something like this is part of the lifestyle of that international group of politicians who can withdraw from anywhere at any time to the center of world democracy as their true home.

## 6.

Politics is also bound by laws; it must adhere to its own essential law if it wants to not only achieve results, but also wants to be successful. Real power is permanent. If it violates the law of its own being, it is doomed to ruin. What we see today is not just the collapse of some democratic states, it is the downfall of the democratic system. Through monumental work, a political genius has brought together all the forces that democracy despised. First and foremost is the power of the generative essence of a people [*Volkstum*]. National Socialism does not criticize democracy's faults, but instead implements a principle of *construction* contrary to the plutocratic principle. At the center of its thinking is the creative man. Pseudo-power of the banks and colonial possessions do not dissuade him from the conviction that in the end it is always *people*, their natural abilities, their work, their diligence, and their spirit, that determine the worth and the endurance of a state. The existence of a state depends solely on the strength of its people — and never on accumulated means of power. States are only changing forms of organization given by peoples. At the core of every nation is a natural, regenerative power in which a deeply hidden, mysterious *will to live* is expressed. Decisive, then, is which direction this will to live takes and what it ultimately accomplishes. Every living force has a certain *qualitatively* determined characteristic. Force is a *qualitative* concept, not *quantitative*. A numerically small people, filled with an indomitable will to live and producing people of high quality and an

---

5    This undoubtedly refers to any of the several "transatlantic crossings" Winston Churchill made during heightened points of the war (e.g., the Atlantic Conference in 1941). These were seen as dishonorable battlefield departures (fleeing) of a leader whose fate should be intertwined with that of his people. [trans.]

extraordinary willingness to act, can nevertheless be superior to a quantitatively stronger people. A disposition to technology, art, and science is of decisive importance for the generative essence of a people [*Volkstum*]. The assertive energy of a people is rooted in the native language and customs, in the sense of justice, in the traditional ways of life and education, in national verse, and in the awareness it has of itself.

A people's vital force does not appear equally at all times. National forces ebb and flow; times of courage and greatness alternate with times of less enterprise. But in the depths, living, creative power persists unshakably; it is indestructible reality from which the national myth draws its strength; it sends the great, representative individuals who appear before their people in order to lead them; it is the sweeping impetus of faith necessary to rouse the world from its "sleep," to bring the deadlocked conditions of power back into harmony with the demands of life.

The forces a real power-politics has to reckon with include the space a people inhabits, the soil they cultivate, and the treasures of natural materials lying dormant in the depths. Space is *never* determining — *man alone* is determining; but favorable terrain, providential borders, fertile soil, and rich mineral resources add an elemental power to the human power that knows how to use them. So out of blood and soil, race and space — those mighty energies of national communities, whose separation and understanding constitute the content of world history — grow.

A politics which ignores or denies these energies — whether they are now made by Freemasons, finance-Jews [*Finanzjuden*], stock-market speculators, ship owners or lords — may well amass riches in individual houses for a few generations; however, such policy harbors the seeds of destruction because it has no connection whatever with constructive forces. Democracy and international capital fight against National Socialism because it is determined to rebuild Europe with those forces ready in every people to end the false rule of money and to establish a new political order based on the generative essence of a people [*Volkstum*].

National Socialism's defining characteristic, which is already beginning to take shape in this war, is the new meaning it gives to *power*. National Socialism puts an end to the confused and destructive theory that power is always simply power and its construction is irrelevant; instead, it teaches that powers should be differentiated. National Socialism affirms every condition of power based on the *natural forces* of a healthy, generative essence of a people [*Volkstum*] and the necessities of the living spaces of peoples. A new age of imperialism is not opened; rather, the age of artificial power-formations [*Machtbildungen*] is closed forever to pave the way for a new age of power — one which is bound by force.

Only vital forces are able to harness power. Left to itself, power is infinite; forces, on the other hand, require actuation, but they never succumb to the *pleonexia* peculiar to power. *Power* is a creation of man, whereas *forces* are a gift of Nature and carry within them the measure of their origin. Man can increase neither his own strength nor the strength of the soil interminably. Life itself advises him not to exploit and exhaust the natural forces, but to live in harmony with them. When a man listens to life's voice, *he* becomes *measured* because he only strives for the *natural* and *healthy*. The mistake of the past was to distrust these forces and ascribe to them an *infinite striving* they do not have. Just as a man is most purely fulfilled when he trusts in life, politics also needs this trust in order to protect itself from tension and excess. By always focusing on living realities first, the politician binds power to force. He goes no further than the vital forces allow; he takes care not to overstretch power for momentary success. Binding power through force means the limitation of power — not by itself, because that is impossible, but by the measure that rests in reality itself.

The politics of binding power through force is the politics of National Socialism. Yet even this policy is not spared conflicts. However, it is a different matter whether conflicts are treated from the standpoint of raw power and, left to themselves, lead to some violent solution, or whether they are mastered in the light of some great and true principle.

Establishing and propagating financial powers discordant with a people's natural strengths has, until now, been a process entangled with short-sighted notions of individual well-being; it has been considered quite pleasant or, at least, harmless. A way of thinking that regards the *nations* as *realities*, and not as mere backdrops for powers alien to blood and soil, on the other hand, recognizes the danger for all in this type of wealth accrual. For an artificial power maintained only by a moneyed class — and not by the generative essence of a people [*Volkstum*] — will naturally seek connection and security with other powers of the same structure. In this way, cross-connections, pacts and pact-systems develop; in short, a political group of money-powers pursuing its own interests prevents all efforts to find objective solutions to ethnic or geopolitical problems because *gold's imperialism does not tolerate any other point of view*. Relations between states are reduced to monetary calculations, capital becomes critical in all decisive questions, international politics becomes completely corrupt.

The political atmosphere is in every sense *detoxified* when the simple and clear power legitimized by force becomes decisive in international relations. A smaller capital has nothing to say to a larger one. Relationships between capital powers are as clear as they are meaningless, since they are purely violent relationships. Pitting *quantities* against each other is always boring. Only when power is carried by an unparalleled, unmistakable, and unalterable force do the relationships between individual powers attain a human character — because the power balance, which is based on a fundamental and natural hierarchy of forces, lacks any incendiary moment. While the smaller quantity lacks any respect for larger quantities, a natural force always asserts its dignity. The weaker force, too, is a revelation of unfathomable being. As *Reichsleiter* Alfred Rosenberg observed in a 13 March 1940 speech in Vienna: a smaller people either never or only reluctantly submits to a people who is comparable in size; but no people keeps its self-respect if, in the living space of a larger people, it ties its fate to the *quantity*. "This people then has the political and moral duty *not* to forcibly transform the soul of the smaller people living in its space and culture. It must honor and respect this folkdom [*Volkstum*], if it proves itself enterprising, as a creation of Nature and history."

Under the rule of democrats, it is forbidden to speak of power at all. Of course, the power relationships in the democratic age were such that it was better not to speak of them. A power as brutal as capital — and the age of *imperialism* is also the age of *capitalism* — *must* work silently. No one needs to hide the power dynamic resulting from natural and historically conditioned forces. There is no reason to suppress the awareness of subjugations if these subjugations are based on the nature of things and never lead to an encroachment on an inherently given dignity and individual character. The fact that a people, in which immense mental and spiritual energies slumber, is able to develop a power that surpasses others cannot deter those who recognize the lawfulness of life. When smaller peoples put themselves under the protection of larger ones, they do not have to pay tribute, as the weaker capital powers do for the stronger ones, but they assert themselves — within the limits set by Nature — in an order the political will creates.

Democracy pretends to be the embodiment of eternal justice. National Socialism despises dishonest phrases. National Socialism trusts in the justice of life, which teaches us to never disparage or disregard struggle, but also to never regard it as an end in itself. Struggle occurs so a more correct order can replace the hollow pseudo-order. Every war has peace as its goal and purpose. Not *peace at any price* and not "eternal" peace, but peace that guarantees every people their existence and room to prosper [*Lebensspielraum*].

A thousand-year-old epoch is coming to an end; Europe lies in the morning light of a rising day. There is no longer any need for the Western "unity" which culminated in such terrible wars. From a *geographical* concept, Europe has become a *political* concept. The young-at-heart gather under a new sign. The unimaginative shuffling of positions of power has forever ended, *a New Order is heralded.* The idea of the nation creates this Order. The living forces of the generative essence of a people [*Volkstum*], which until now could only develop politically in a hindered and broken manner by the universal Western ideology, are gaining free space for the first time. The New Order is not based on a new "ideology," but on *the realities through which the nations were created.* On a firm foundation common to all, new structures of states will arise. They are *enlivened by the idea of the nation*, which, as reality is to imagination, is superior to any mere *ideology. Enlivened*, they are limited by the principle that all genuine power must correspond to the living forces carrying them. The New Order carries its principle within itself; its inner measure is one with the justice of being.

# OTHER BOOKS PUBLISHED BY ARKTOS

# OTHER BOOKS PUBLISHED BY ARKTOS

# OTHER BOOKS PUBLISHED BY ARKTOS

| | |
|---|---|
| EDGAR JULIUS JUNG | *The Significance of the German Revolution* |
| RUUBEN KAALEP & AUGUST MEISTER | *Rebirth of Europe* |
| RODERICK KAINE | *Smart and SeXy* |
| PETER KING | *Here and Now* |
| | *Keeping Things Close* |
| | *On Modern Manners* |
| JAMES KIRKPATRICK | *Conservatism Inc.* |
| LUDWIG KLAGES | *The Biocentric Worldview* |
| | *Cosmogonic Reflections* |
| | *The Science of Character* |
| ANDREW KORYBKO | *Hybrid Wars* |
| PIERRE KREBS | *Guillaume Faye: Truths & Tributes* |
| | *Fighting for the Essence* |
| JULIEN LANGELLA | *Catholic and Identitarian* |
| JOHN BRUCE LEONARD | *The New Prometheans* |
| STEPHEN PAX LEONARD | *The Ideology of Failure* |
| | *Travels in Cultural Nihilism* |
| WILLIAM S. LIND | *Reforging Excalibur* |
| | *Retroculture* |
| PENTTI LINKOLA | *Can Life Prevail?* |
| H. P. LOVECRAFT | *The Conservative* |
| NORMAN LOWELL | *Imperium Europa* |
| RICHARD LYNN | *Sex Differences in Intelligence* |
| | *A Tribute to Helmut Nyborg* (ed.) |
| JOHN MACLUGASH | *The Return of the Solar King* |
| CHARLES MAURRAS | *The Future of the Intelligentsia &* |
| | *For a French Awakening* |
| JOHN HARMON MCELROY | *Agitprop in America* |
| MICHAEL O'MEARA | *Guillaume Faye and the Battle of Europe* |
| | *New Culture, New Right* |
| MICHAEL MILLERMAN | *Beginning with Heidegger* |
| DMITRY MOISEEV | *The Philosophy of Italian Fascism* |
| MAURICE MURET | *The Greatness of Elites* |
| BRIAN ANSE PATRICK | *The NRA and the Media* |
| | *Rise of the Anti-Media* |
| | *The Ten Commandments of Propaganda* |
| | *Zombology* |
| TITO PERDUE | *The Bent Pyramid* |
| | *Journey to a Location* |
| | *Lee* |
| | *Morning Crafts* |
| | *Philip* |
| | *The Sweet-Scented Manuscript* |
| | *William's House* (vol. 1–4) |
| JOHN K. PRESS | *The True West vs the Zombie Apocalypse* |
| RAIDO | *A Handbook of Traditional Living* (vol. 1–2) |

# OTHER BOOKS PUBLISHED BY ARKTOS

www.ingramcontent.com/pod-product-compliance
Lightning Source LLC
Chambersburg PA
CBHW021400090426
42742CB00009B/938